Tort Law Q&A

Private Law Tutor Publishing

Foreword

Thank you for buying this book. The problem that I encountered when studying law is: knowing everything. There is so much to read and so little time to do it. If you skip some material, or a case you are none the wiser. So throughout my years teaching law I have devised a system and I am going to share this with you.

You may have encountered different methods or formulas to help when advising a client in a mock scenario. One of example is the *IRAC* method or another is *Celo*. These are well documented and you can read about these. I never used them, because I had a method in my head that worked. It was not until I started teaching that I spoke about it. I call my method the "**Fact Law Sandwich**". Let me explain. If you are asked to advise a party as to their legal rights this is how you present it:

FACTS
GENERAL PRINCIPLE
LAW
APPLY TO FACTS

In **Fact:** simply state what you have been told, this why you can never be accused of not considering the facts. In **General principle:** you simply state what the general rule of the relevant issue is. You express it as if you are speaking to a child who has no knowledge of law. In **Law**: you state "using the authority of.....and you go on to state which statute or case helps prove your point. Lastly in **Apply to Facts**: you apply the reasoning of the case to your factual scenario. Your advice will sound and look structured and professional. The reason it is called the "Fact Law Sandwich", is because the advice contains two outer layers of facts that sandwich the principle and law in the middle.

This book is written to provide the student with a good knowledge of the most important cases on their study. It is written in a way to facilitate the Fact Law Sandwich method. I provide the general principle, the name of the case with full citation, the facts, the Ratio (the thing the lecturers say you always need to use), and application i.e. how the case should be applied. No other book provides this information at your fingertips. I hope you enjoy using it.

Tort Law Q&A
Private Law Tutor Publishing

Chapter 1 - Welcome/Introduction/Overview

This book provides you with basic information as a basis for you to form your own critical opinions on this area of law. Once you have mastered the basics, you will be inspired to question principles in your essays and apply them in mock client advisory scenarios. Again, for your convenience, we have provided you with examples of how to answer such questions and how to apply your knowledge as effectively as possible to help you get the best possible marks. This aid is a fully-fledged source of basic information, which tries to give the student comprehensive understanding of how to answer questions for this module.

The aim of this Book is to:

- Provide an introduction to anyone studying or interested in studying Law to the key principles and concepts that exist in this module.
- To provide a framework to consider the law in this module within the context of examinations or written work.
- Provide a detailed learning resource in order for legal written examination skills to be developed.
- Facilitate the development of written and critical thinking skills.
- Promote the practice of problem solving skills.
- To establish a platform for students to gain a solid understanding of the basic principles and concepts of in this module, this can then be expanded upon through confident independent learning.

Through this Book, students will be able to demonstrate the ability to:

- Demonstrate an awareness of the core principles;
- Critically assess challenging mock factual scenarios and be able to pick out legal issues in the various

areas of this module;

- Apply their knowledge when writing a formal assessment;
- Present a reasoned argument and make a judgment on competing viewpoints;
- Make use of technical legalistic vocabulary in the appropriate manner; and
- Be responsible for their learning process and work in an adaptable and flexible way.

Studying this module

This question and answer series covers core subjects that the Law Society and the Bar Council deem essential in a qualifying law degree. Therefore, it is vital that a student successfully pass these subjects to become a lawyer. The primary method by which your understanding of the law will develop is by understanding how to solve problem questions. You will also be given essay questions in your examinations. The methods by which these types of question should be approached are somewhat different.

Tackling Problems and Essay Questions

There are various ways of approaching problem questions and essay questions. We have provided students with an in-depth analysis with suggested questions and answers.

Chapter 2 - Duty of Care

Question

'You must take reasonable care to avoid acts or omissions which you can reasonably foresee would be likely to injure your neighbour. Who, then, in law is my neighbour? The answer seems to be - persons who are so closely and directly affected by my act that I ought reasonably to have them in contemplation as being so affected when I am directing my mind to the acts or omissions which are called in question.' (Lord Atkin in *Donoghue v Stevenson* [1932] AC 562, p. 580).

Critically review Lord Atkin's famous dictum and assess to what extent the English courts have developed the law on the duty of care in the modern law of negligence.

Answer

The best modern definition of Tort comes from Percy H Winfield in *The Province of the Law of Tort* as *'Tortious liability arises from the breach of a duty primarily fixed by the law: such duty is towards persons generally and its breach is redressible by an action for unliquidated damages.'*[1]

The Neighbour test was developed by the courts and represents the first test applied in order to assess the presence of a duty of care. Judges started moving towards the formulation of a general principle of duty of care.[2] The quote in the question by Lord Atkin in <u>Donoghue v Stevenson</u>[3] was the first legal formulation of duty of care to identify negligence: The Neighbour's test. The principle established that a manufacturer owed a duty of care to the ultimate consumer. The absence of a contract between the parties did

---

[1] Percy, H., Winfield, *The Province of the Law of Tort* (first published 1931, CUP, 2013): 32

[2] Heaven v Pender [1883] 11 QBD 503

[3] Lord Atkin in Donoghue v Stevenson [1932] AC 562, p. 580

not exclude the presence of duty of care against the manufacturer.

There has been a significant development of the concept of duty of care, which stemmed from the Neighbour test. There was an introduction of the concept of duty of care in relation to economic loss caused by negligent misstatement.[4] There was an introduction of the concept of duty of care in relation to tortious actions committed by a third party.[5] There was a modern reformulation of Lord Atkin's 'Neighbour principle' in Anns v London Borough of Merton.[6] Lord Wilberforce attempted to lay down an approach which could be applied in all situations in order to determine the existence of a duty of care. A two-stage test was reformulated: 1) between the parties involved there must be a sufficient relationship of proximity or neighbourhood that will likely cause damage to another person; and 2) are there any policy reasons why no duty of care should be considered to be owed?

The Anns test opened the floodgates. It was applied to the very close relationship between two parties which may cause the presence of a quasi-contractual relationship that justifies the presence of duty of care.[7] A better explanation was provided by the court on the element of 'proximity' to reduce the scope of duty of care and avoid floodgates.[8] The court decided to adopt a narrower approach in order to avoid floodgates. The courts held a claim in negligence requires the person to be the legal owner or the possessor in title of the property at the time of the damage.[9] Finally the two-stage test in Anns was

---

[4] Hedley Byrne & Co. Ltd v Heller and Partners [1963] AC 465

[5] Home Office v Dorset Yacht Co. [1970] AC 1004

[6] Anns v London Borough of Merton [1978] AC 728

[7] Junior Books v Veitchi Co. Ltd [1983] 21 BLR 66

[8] Sutherland Shire Council v Heyman (1985) 60 ALR 1 (Australian case)

[9] Leigh & Sillivan Ltd v Aliakmon Shipping Co Ltd [1986] AC 785

rejected to restrain the identification of duty of care.[10] The courts said foreseeability of harm is a necessary ingredient of a duty of care relationship. *'Otherwise there would be liability in negligence on the part of one who sees another about to walk over a cliff with his head in the air, and forbears to shout a warning'.* It was in the context of the retreat from Anns that emphasis was placed in a number of cases on the concept of "proximity", and on the idea that it must be fair to impose a duty of care on the defendant.[11]

In order to avoid a floodgate of claims and to give structure to the identification of duty of care, the court moved away from the position in <u>Donoghue</u> and <u>Anns</u> whereby foreseeability of damage was enough to make a claim in negligence. They introduced the Caparo three-stage test.[12] The Caparo-three stage test represents the actual state of the law in identifying duty of care. Three elements are needed to identify a duty of care: 1) Foreseeability – was the loss caused by the Defendant to the Claimant reasonably foreseeable? 2) Proximity – Is there legal closeness between the parties at the time the Defendant was negligent? and 3) Fair, just and reasonable – Is it fair, just and reasonable to impose a duty to the Defendant? The last question has been seen as a residual discretion left to the court in deciding the imposition of a duty). Lord Bridge noted that decisions after Anns had emphasised *"the inability of any single general principle to provide a practical test which can be applied to every situation."[13]*

The 'incremental approach' represents the main theory applied by the courts to identify the existence of duty of care.

---

[10] Yuen Kun-Yeu v Attorney-General of Hong Kong [1987] 2 All ER 705

[11] Lord Oliver of Aylmerton, Judicial Legislation: Retreat from Anns, presented at The 3rd Sultan Azlan Shah 12 Law Lecture, p 53, 1988 September 12

[12] Caparo Industries plc v Dickman [1990] UKHL 2; [1990] 2 A.C. 605

[13] [1990] 2 A.C. 605, p.617

Accordingly a duty of care exists in those situations that can be regarded as analogous to one in which a duty of care has already been recognised. In order to establish the presence of duty of care firstly, it has to be checked whether there is any existing legal authority for a duty of care in circumstances similar to the one under examination. If there is a duty recognised by earlier cases, then the court can follow them. However, when recognising and developing an established category, the courts are being influenced by policy considerations.[14] If there is no existing legal authority, then the Caparo three-stage test should be used.

In order to establish the presence of duty of care all the three following requirements are necessary: i) foreseeability, ii) proximity and iii) fair, just and reasonable policy considerations.[15] The law attributes a duty of care between employers and their employees.[16] Even if the damage is foreseeable and there is proximity between the parties, the imposition of duty of care must be fair, just and reasonable.[17]

It was in any event made clear in <u>Michael v Chief Constable of South Wales Police</u>[18] that the idea that Caparo established a tripartite test is mistaken. Properly understood, Caparo thus achieves a balance between legal certainty and justice. In cases where the question whether a duty of care arises has not previously been decided, the courts will consider the closest analogies in the existing law, with a view to maintaining the coherence of the law and the avoidance of inappropriate distinctions. They will also weigh up the reasons for and against imposing liability, in order to decide whether the existence of a duty of care would be just and reasonable.

---

[14] Lord Reid, 'The Judge as Lawmaker (1972)' *Journal of the Society of Public Teachers of Law* 12 (1995), 22
[15] Watson v British Boxing Board of Control Ltd [2001] QB 1134

[16] Spring v Guardian Assurance plc & Others [1995] 2 AC 296
[17] Marc Rich & Co AG v Bishop Rock Marine Co Ltd (The Nicholas H) [1996] AC 211
[18] [2015] UKSC 2; [2015] AC 1732

In <u>Robinson v Chief Constable of West Yorkshire</u>[19] Mrs Robinson was walking down a street. In the same street Police officers were detaining a suspected drug dealer. The suspect put up resistance and moved up the street. The Claimant was knocked to the ground and injured. The Court of Appeal dismissed the Claimant's arguments. It had not been fair, just and reasonable to impose a duty of care. The interest of the public may outweigh the interests of the single individual. The case was appealed to the Supreme Court.[20] The Supreme Court made significant inroads into the principle that the police cannot be sued in negligence save in exceptional circumstances as a result of alleged failures in their core operational duties. The Court stressed that there is no single definitive test that should be used to assess whether a duty of care will arise in any particular case. Rather, what is required is: "[A]*n approach based, in the manner characteristic of the common law, on precedent, and on the development of the law incrementally and by analogy with established authorities*".

The Court reviewed the evolution of the law on the imposition of duties of care. It is thus essential reading for tort lawyers. It is self-evident that any case which includes express reference to (amongst others) <u>Donoghue v Stevenson</u>, <u>Hedley Byrne v Heller</u>, <u>Anns v Merton</u>, <u>Murphy v Brentwood</u>, <u>Caparo v Dickman</u>, <u>Stovin v Wise</u> is going to be of importance.

The Supreme Court went on to say *"[I]t is neither necessary nor appropriate to treat <u>Caparo</u> as requiring the application of its familiar three-stage examination afresh to every action brought. Where the law is clear that a particular relationship, or recurrent factual situation, gives rise to a duty of care, there is no occasion to resort to Caparo, at least unless the court is being invited to depart from previous authority"*.[21]

---

[19] Robinson v Chief Constable of West Yorkshire [2014] EWCA Civ 15

[20] Robinson v Chief Constable of West Yorkshire Police [2018] UKSC 4

[21] Robinson v Chief Constable of West Yorkshire Police [2018]

What the *Supreme Court* is saying is where the lower courts have already determined whether a duty of care should be imposed in particular circumstances, there is no need for this issue to be reconsidered in subsequent cases. It is surprising that the court would imposed on the police in this case a duty of care, given the long and consistent line of high authority which appeared to have been stated in firm terms that no such duty arises should be imposed on the police public policy grounds. However, the reassurance inherent in the incremental approach assumes that the existing law is properly understood. In <u>Robinson</u>, the Supreme Court decided that various statements of the law in this area – including from the Supreme Court itself – were not correct, or at least had not been properly understood.

Conclusion

Tort law bases on the idea that a person owes a duty of care to another individual. The breach of this duty may give rise to liability. A legal duty to take care is where care should be taken to ensure a person should not be exposed to *"liability in an indeterminate amount for an indeterminate time to an indeterminate class"*. First, you have to prove the existence of a duty of care. The Neighbour test represents the first test applied in order to assess the presence of a duty of care. There was a significant development of the concept of duty of care, stemmed from the Neighbour test. The court decided to adopt a narrower approach due to the avoidance of floodgates. In order to avoid a flood of claims and to give structure to the identification of duty of care, the court introduced the <u>Caparo</u> three-stage test. According to the so-called 'incremental approach' a duty of care will exist in a situation which can be regarded as analogous to one in which a duty of care has already been found. In cases where the question whether a duty of care arises has not previously been decided, the courts will consider the closest analogies in the existing law, with a view to maintaining the coherence of the law and the

---

UKSC 4, 100

avoidance of inappropriate distinctions.

Chapter 3 - Restricted duties, Omissions & Acts of 3rd Parties

Problem Question

To celebrate his 35th birthday, Alf, an army doctor, goes drinking with a young corporal Will, who he knows to be an alcoholic with a dangerously low capacity to restrain himself. He warns Will twice during the (long) evening of drinking that he is drinking too much, but Will does not listen. Will then collapses into a coma. Alf, who is himself intoxicated, fails in his attempt to give Will some first aid. He delays before calling an ambulance, wondering whether the incident might damage his army career. Even after the call, there is a long delay before the ambulance arrives. Will dies on the way to hospital. It is established that if either Alf had summoned the ambulance earlier, or if the ambulance had arrived promptly when summoned, the Will would probably have lived. The ambulance services claim that their crew arrived late at the scene of the accident because they got lost. It was established that driving conditions that night were dangerous and visibility was poor as a result of heavy rain.

Advise the following parties: Alf, the local ambulance services and Will's relatives.

Answer

This paper will start with a brief introduction of the approach adopted by the law in relation to the negligence claims. It will then analyse both potential liabilities of the parties involved in the scenario, such as Alf and the ambulance service. The paper will end with the apportionment of the potential damages owed by the parties to the Claimant.

Introduction

The tort of negligence bases on the idea that a person owes a duty of care to another individual. The breach of this duty may give rise to liability. The initial approach adopted by the court towards negligence claims based on a case-by-case analysis. Later on, the law developed a proper test to ascertain the presence of a valid duty of care between the parties involved. The first formulation of this rule stems from the case **Donoghue v Stevenson** [1932] AC 562, in which the neighbour's principle was established. The court set out the presence of a duty of care that everyone owes towards his or her neighbours. Everyone must take reasonable care in order to avoid acts or omissions that can reasonably foresee would be likely to injure someone. Subsequently, the law found fundamental to set out a proper test in order to establish the presence of a valid duty of care. The leading case is **Caparo Industries plc v Dickman** [1990] UKHL 2. The test adopted by the court based on the identification of three elements: foreseeability, proximity and fair, just and reasonable imposition. The court will assess whether the loss suffered by the Claimant was reasonably foreseeable, since between the parties there was legal closeness and the imposition of the duty results fair, just and reasonable. In order to succeed in a negligence claim, all the three criteria must be satisfied.

Nevertheless, in some peculiar circumstances the approach can be influenced by specific rules. These rules relate to cases involving restricted duty situations, omissions and acts of third parties.

Alf's liability

The first issue is whether Alf is liable for failure to have provided proper first aid to his fellow and for the delay in calling the ambulance. Alf is an army doctor that goes drinking with Will, a young corporal that he knows to be an alcoholic with a dangerously low capacity to restrain himself. Notwithstanding the two warnings Alf gave to him, Will drank too much and collapsed into a coma. Alf was intoxicated and failed in his attempt to give Will first aid. This part of the scenario relates to two specific areas of the tort of negligence, which are omissions, and assumption of responsibility.

According to the general rule adopted by courts towards omissions, the law does not impose a duty to intervene to prevent someone from suffering an injury. The Defendant does not owe a duty of care in respect of omissions as stated in the American case of **Osterling v Hill** [1928], where the Claimant drowned after renting a canoe that overturned. The Defendant was an expert swimmer, but he did not intervene. He was not responsible. Individuals that are injured by omission to do something do not have right of compensation. Nevertheless, the law may impose a duty of care in some peculiar circumstances where the Defendant, even without acting, is involved. The three exceptions to the general rule are:

1.   Whether the Defendant exercises a degree of control towards the situation;
2.   Whether there is assumption of responsibility by the Defendant; and
3.   Whether the Defendant has contributed to the creation of the risk.

The second exception of assumption of responsibility is the most significant to analyse the scenario. Assumption of responsibility may derive from an employment relationship between the parties or by looking at the conduct of the Defendant. According to the employment relationship rule, there is a duty between work fellows to help each other. This has been expressed in the case **Costello v Chief Constable of Northumbria Police** [1998] EWCA Civ 1898 where a prisoner attacked a police constable and the police inspector in the vicinity did not intervene. On the other side, the case **Barrett v MOD** [1995] 1 WL 1217 attributed liability to the Defendant that failed in supervising a drunk pilot, taken to his bedroom due to intoxication for alcohol. In its reasoning, the Court of Appeal pointed out that the Defendant did not breach his duty for lack of control over the pilots when they were drinking. It is fair, just and reasonable for the law to leave a responsible adult to assume responsibility for his own actions in consuming alcohol. The court explained that the liability of the Defendant arose from another point. By taking the drunken pilot to his bedroom, the Defendant assumed responsibility towards his safety. Whether the omission to do so would have not given rise to liability, the conduct of the Defendant leads to the conclusion that he has assumed responsibility in respect of the situation.

The same reasoning may be applied to the scenario. Alf has attempted to give Will first aid. His conduct leads to the outcome that he has assumed responsibility towards the young caporal. His delay in calling the ambulance has compromised his safety. Therefore, Alf has breached the duty of care arisen from his assumption of responsibility. The court will likely take into account, as in **Barrett v MOD** the contributory negligence element represented by the lack of self-control of the disease in assessing compensation.

Ambulance service

The issue related to the intervention of the ambulance relates to those restricted duty situations established by the law. Special rules have been developed for those cases involving liability of public bodies. Public bodies will be liable in negligence only where their actions have made the situation in which they intervene worse. For instance, as a matter of policy, the police have a duty to concentrate all its effort and resources on the collective welfare and not on single individuals. Therefore, as in **Hill v Chief Constable of West Yorkshire** [1989] 2 WLR 1049, the police that could not prevent the death of the Claimant's daughter was not liable for not having focused all its resources on that particular victim.

The approach adopted by the court will be different in relation to two peculiar bodies such as the fire brigade and the ambulance. Whether it can be showed that these two authorities by their intervention have worsened the situation, they may be held liable. The present scenario involves an ambulance. By definition, the ambulance service represents an extension of the National Health Service that legally owes a duty of care towards its patients, unless specific policy considerations arise. In the case of **Kent v Griffiths** [2002] 2 WLR 1158, a GP received a call by the Claimant, a pregnant woman, that was having an asthma attack. The GP called the ambulance few times and the ambulance arrived 38 minutes late. The woman lost her baby and she suffered psychiatric injuries. When assessing the liability of the ambulance service, the court analysed whether the Defendant had reasons to arrive late. There were no reasons, but the ambulance service tried to argue that, as a public body, they did not owe a duty of care to the woman. The court disagreed. The Defendant was responsible since the ambulance service owed a duty to respond to the call and give a prompt service.

As much as in the case of Kent v Griffith, the ambulance in the scenario has arrived late to the scene so that Will have died on the way to the hospital. The death was the result of the late call made by Alf and due to the late arrival of the ambulance itself. Nevertheless, evidence showed that driving conditions that night were dangerous and visibility was poor because of heavy rain. Differently than **Kent v Griffith**, the ambulance had reasons for being late that may justify its failure to give prompt intervention. The safety of the people on the ambulance counts as much as the safety of a patient therefore it is reasonable to expect the ambulance to drive carefully due to the danger of driving that night. Getting lost due to the natural conditions of that night may justify the delay. Whether the ambulance proved that they have intervened as soon as the call was received so that they have complied with the duty expected such as answering to the call and giving prompt service, they will likely escape liability. The court may also decide to simply reduce the compensation awarded, considering the peculiar forecast conditions of that night, but still holding the ambulance liable. This may happen whether the court will be not persuaded that getting lost was strictly related to the heavy rain. One thing is driving carefully due to the dangerous night so that the ambulance is late. Another thing is getting lost.

Apportionment of damages

Assuming that the court considered both Alf and the ambulance responsible due to the delay that has caused Will's death, the court will need to apportion liability between the Defendants. The starting point will be that each Defendant is 50 per cent liable. Nevertheless, the court will likely reduce the compensation owed to Will's relatives by considering the lack of self-control of the disease and the climate conditions of that night. In **Barrett v MOD** [1995] 1 WL 1217, the court attributed 25 per cent of responsibility to the drunk pilot so that it is reasonable to assume the same reduction in the compensation owed by Alf. The same percentage will be attributed to the consideration of the climate conditions that have caused the delay of the ambulance.

Chapter 4 - Psychiatric Harm

Problem Question

"It may be said that the common law should not pay attention to these feelings about the relative merits of different classes of claimants. It should stick to principle and not concern itself with distributive justice. An extension of liability to rescuers and helpers would be a modest an incremental development in the common law tradition and, as between these plaintiffs and these defendants, produce a just result. My Lords, I disagree. It seems to be that in this area of the law, the search for principle was called off in Alcock v Chief Constable of South Yorkshire [1992] 1 A.C. 310. No one can pretend that the existing law which your Lordships have to accept, is founded upon principle." Per Lord Hoffman in White v Chief Constable of South Yorkshire [1999] 2 A.C. 455 at 511

Evaluate this statement and assess whether the claims of the policemen should have been successful as an incremental development of the law on negligently caused psychiatric injury. Your answer should also discuss whether this area of the law has achieved the correct balance between principle and ideas of distributive justice. Introduction

Answer

Introduction

The paper will start by setting the question into context. Second, this paper will examine the current state of the law in relation to negligently caused psychiatric injury. Third, this paper will then examine the restriction placed on secondary victims. Fourth, this paper will assess whether the claims of rescuers or employees like in **White v Chief Constable of South Yorkshire**[22] should have been successful and whether the law should incrementally extended the duty of care to

---

[22] [1999] 2 A.C. 455 at 511

secondary victims. Fifth, this paper examines what possible reforms can be introduced. Lastly, this paper examines whether this area of the law has achieved the correct balance between principle and ideas of distributive justice.

The general principles for deciding if a duty of care exists in a case involving negligently caused psychiatric injury is not straightforward. The courts in this area have adopted different approaches. The way they have done this is by imposing further conditions or criteria that must be satisfied before they are willing to accept a duty of care has arisen. When deciding if a duty of care exists, the court evaluates the 'floodgates' principle. This refers to the idea that the imposition of liability on defendants might prove uncontrollable and unnecessarily burdensome. Therefore, the courts feel they must make it harder for Claimants to establish the existence of a duty of care.[23] This in turn has been criticized as *"the area where the silliest rules now exist"*. [24]

The Current law

In **Page v Smith**[25] the House of Lords highlighted that foreseeability of psychiatric illness was not the correct test. Where a claimant had been *"directly involved in the accident"* and *"well within the range of foreseeable physical injury"*, he would be looked at as a "primary", opposed to a "secondary" victim". This would mean a primary victim would be owed the same duty of care which applies in cases concerning physical harm. Lord Lloyd said that it is essential in all claims relating to psychiatric illness to make this classification.

More recent cases have confirmed the validity of this classification.[26] Lord Oliver, in **Alcock v Chief Constable of**

---

[23] P R Handford, "Compensation for Psychiatric Injury: The Limits of Liability" (1995) 2 Psychiatry, Psychology and Law 37

[24] Dr J Stapleton, "In Restraint of Tort" in P Birks (ed), *The Frontiers of Liability* (1994) vol 2, pp 94-96

[25] [1996] A.C. 155

[26] Frost v Chief Constable of South Yorkshire Police [1997] 3

South Yorkshire Police[27] further developed this distinction by saying "primary" victims are involved, *"either mediately or immediately"*, as a participant in the event created by the defendant's negligence' and a "secondary" victim is "simply a passive and unwilling witness of injury caused to others".[28] He further stated primary victims where (i) claimant who feared for their own safety; (ii) rescuers; and (iii) involuntary participants.

The Restriction on Secondary Victims

In **Alcock** claims were brought by relatives and friends of some of the people killed in a crush at the Hillsborough football stadium in Sheffield after the police had negligently allowed a crowd to build up too rapidly in a particular part of the stand. The House of Lords reviewed the law on the scope of liability for psychiatric injury, and clarified three points.

First, they said, there must be a sufficiently close relationship of love and affection between claimant and the person killed or injured to make it reasonably foreseeable that the claimant would suffer psychiatric injury in the circumstances. Second, the House upheld the requirement of proximity in time. If the claimant is on the scene of the accident and sees or hears it happen, that certainly suffices, as it does if he comes upon the "immediate aftermath" as allowed in the case of **McLoughlin**, though the House declined to define that phrase any more precisely. Third, the House confirmed that P must have seen or heard the accident or its immediate aftermath at first hand. A person who saw a news report of the accident or who was told about it by a third party would have no claim; even those who had been watching the live broadcast from Hillsbrough were not eligible, since the TV pictures did not show the suffering of recognisable individuals.

WLR 1194 at 1203; Hegarty v EE Caledonia Ltd [1997] 2 Lloyd's Rep 259 at 265-266
May 1997;
[27] [1992] 1 AC 310
[28] [1992] 1 AC 310 at 407

Jones argues that the distinction between a primary and secondary victim does not stand up to analysis. Furthermore, the distinction, while being a rationalisation of the present state of the law, does not provide any justification for the different liability rules that are applied.[29]

Rescuers and Employees

The classification of rescuers and employees has caused the courts some problems and they have been inconsistent in their approach when deciding these types of case.[30] Rescuers are not given any special status in this area of law and they must be classified like all other claimants.[31]

The question for the court in **White v Chief Constable of South Yorkshire**[32] was whether their Lordships should apply the incremental step of extending liability for psychiatric injury to rescuers. The court looked at the case of **Chadwick v British Railways Board**[33] where the claimant witnessed aftermath of a major crash situation, while assisting in the rescue of victims. He became psycho-neurotic as a result. It has been observed that the claimant in this case was actually a primary victim. The court put the rescuer into the artificial legal category of "primary" victim exempting the control mechanisms. Waller J. said that it was foreseeable that *"somebody might try to rescue passengers and suffer injury in the process."* and *"shock was foreseeable and . . . rescue was foreseeable."*[34] Thus the judge's reasoning is based purely

---

[29] M A Jones, "Liability for Psychiatric Illness - More Principle, Less Subtlety?" [1995] 4 Web JCLI

[30] K J Nasir, "Nervous Shock and *Alcock*: The Judicial Buck Stops Here" (1992) 55 MLR 705

[31] F A Trindade, "The Principles Governing the Recovery of Damages for Negligently Caused Nervous Shock" [1986] CLJ 476, 485-495

[32] [1999] 2 A.C. 455 at 511

[33] [1967] 1 WLR 912

[34] [1967] 1 WLR 912 at 921

upon the foreseeability. This is questionable because the claimant's psychiatric illness came as a reaction to the events he had witnessed, involving injury to others but no fear of injury to him.

Similarly, in *Wigg v British Railways Board*,[35] a train driver who tried to rescue someone trapped under a train recovered compensation. This is because he was himself in danger and suffered the nervous shock as a result of fearing for his own safety. In **Wigg**, Tucker J. expressly said that the only question was that of foreseeability, referring to the speech of Lord Bridge of Harwich in **McLoughlin**.[36]

In **Dooley v. Cammell Laird & Co. Ltd**.[37] a cable of a crane snapped and load fell onto the ground. The crane operator thought his fellow employees below would be injured and he suffered psychiatric injury. In **Galt v. British Railways Board** [38] the claimant suffered shock and consequent heart problems, when the train he was driving nearly hit two men working by the lines. In both of these cases the courts felt it was right to make the defendants liable, thus throwing the claimant into a category of primary victim, with no reference to the control mechanisms, which had not yet been invented at that time.

In *White v Chief Constable of the South Yorkshire Police*[39] the claimants were police officers on duty during the Hillsborough football stadium disaster. They had assisted in removing the dead bodies and carrying the injured to safety as well as trying to resuscitate spectators. Their action was for Post-Traumatic Stress Disorder as a result of these experiences. They claimed both as employees and as professional rescuers. The House of Lords dismissed their appeal. The Claimants argument can be summed up in Lord

---

[35] (1986) 136 NLJ 446

[36] [1983] 1 A.C. 410

[37] [1951] 1 Lloyd's L.R. 271

[38] [1983] 113 N.L.J. 870

[39] [1999] 2 A.C. 455

Goff dissenting comment:

> *"What rescuer ever thinks of his own safety? It seems to me that it would be a very artificial and unnecessary control, to say a rescuer can only recover if he was in fact in physical danger. A danger to which he probably never gave thought, and which in the event might not cause physical injury."*

The claimants relied on the abovementioned authorities of **Dooley;**[40] **Wiggs;**[41] and **Galt**[42]. Lord Hoffman dismissed these authorities on the basis they were *"ex tempore first instance judgments given on circuit."* For Lord Hoffman, these decisions were regarded as cases raising questions of fact, namely whether psychiatric injury to the claimant was a foreseeable consequence of the defendant's negligent conduct. It was in accordance with the law (post **Alcock**) as it was thought to be at the time.

For the House of Lords, the claimant's status as employees did not automatically convert them from secondary victims to primary victims. The ordinary criteria of nervous shock as set out in **Alcock** applied. The claimant's argument as to being professional rescuers failed in that they had not actually been exposed to danger themselves. The claimant's employment argument also failed. Their Lordships felt the employment relationship does not mean employee is a primary victim. As for the employer's implied contractual duty not to cause harm, this is no greater than that imposed by the ordinary law of tort. The court felt while the police were entitled to sympathy their claims were no greater than those of others such as doctors and other hospital workers, and in this case particularly bereaved relatives to whom the law denied redress. Mullany and Handford [43] have argued House of Lords' decision in

---

[40] [1951] 1 Lloyd's L.R. 271
[41] The Times, 4 February 1986
[42] [1983] 113 N.L.J. 870
[43] N J Mullany and P R Handford, "Hillsborough Replayed" (1997)

Alcock has brought about the wrong result.

Policy decision making

The question which arises is: Why the courts felt it was right to deny this class of claimant? The reason is that the court is making a policy decision. The courts do not want a proliferation of similar claims to come to court (the floodgate principle). This is seen by Lord Wilberforce's dicta in **McLoughlin v O'Brian**.[44] In addition, Lord Wilberforce stated the extension may lead to possibly fraudulent claims by lawyers and psychiatrists who will formulate a claim for nervous shock damages, namely customary miscarriage, as it is termed in America. Lord Wilberforce goes on to say liability would be an unfair burden to defendants, and then ultimately insurance companies. Thirdly, this would produce evidentiary difficulties and tend to lengthen litigation. Fourthly, Lord Wilberforce believed that an extension of the scope of liability ought only to be made by the legislature. It is argued the abovementioned can not form the basis of legal decision making and rejection of the incremental development of the law on negligently caused psychiatric injury. Judges deciding cases based on policy factors informing their decisions is wrong.

The UK system is built on the separation of powers, where the judiciary is independent and politically neutral. Judges are theoretical supposed to interpret the law in a way parliament intended, but there is a lot of discretion available to judges to bend the law to what they believe is just. Judges are not elected lawmakers and should not have the power to legislate. Consideration of policy, it can be argued disturbs the separation of the courts from the organs of the state.

Reforms

---

113 LQR 410, 417
[44] [1983] 1 A.C. 410 at 421

The law on liability for psychiatric illness has attracted some sharp criticisms. In order to rectify the inconsistent approach, we firstly can abolish all liability for psychiatric illness in the absence of physical injury. This has however been rejected by the Law Commission.[45] Secondly we can leave the present rules on recovery as they are; this has also been rejected. Third we can amend some of the most arbitrary rules, generally by removing restrictions on recovery thereby extending liability, though retaining some restrictions; The Law Commission has taken the provisional view that this option is the appropriate route. Lastly, Mullany and Handford have suggested we treat liability for psychiatric illness in exactly the same way as liability for physical injury. [46] The House of Lords have confirmed damages can be recovered for physical injury suffered by a professional rescuer[47] and it is difficult to see why psychiatric injury should be treated any differently.

The theory of Distributive Justice

John Rawls in his book *A Theory of Justice*[48] steppes outside the general narrow idea of law and its interpretation, and produces a theory of social justice. He looks at the law, but at the same time looks at the broad structure of society, trying to create a theory of justice. He does not consider analytical questions over what law is. Rather, he imagines if we were to start society again, how we would create a just one. It is a political theory which asks legal questions.

Rawls basically 'pretends' to find out what may work. He invented some imaginary friends who would be faced with complicated problems. They would be put into the *original position*. This is where there is no society. The people in the

---

[45] *Law Commission, Liability for Psychiatric Illness, (1998), LC249 at* http://www.lawcom.gov.uk/docs/lc249(1).pdf

[46] Mullany and Handford, The Liability for Psychiatric Damage (Sydney: 1993)

[47] Ogwo v Taylor [1988] AC 431

[48] J Rawls, A Theory of Justice. Cambridge, Massachusetts: Belknap Press of Harvard University Press, 1971.

original position are the architects of a brand new society. This is difficult because Rawls blindfolds all of these people. He calls his blindfold *the veil of ignorance*. This means that these people know nothing about themselves. They are only allowed to know two things: an objective and a subjective condition. The former is that they know the society they will design has a moderate scarcity of resources. The latter is they are told that they are rational and that they are mutually disinterested.

Rawls did this in order to come up with principles that would be suitable for anybody in society. He makes these people behind the veil anybody. He wanted to design a theory that would cater for everyone, which everyone would agree to. He did not want to make the error that Aristotle did.[49] Furthermore, he wants it to be stable and timeless. He wanted to create a theory which respects that fact that everyone is individual and distinct.

Using Rawls theory, we can see that the courts by creating this distinction between primary and secondary victims are doing just this. Sometimes a rule will not benefit everyone. And if a class of claimants such as rescuers will be unsuccessful, then this will be an adequate price to pay for not overburdening the defendant and ultimately insurers. The big criticism of this is by the *communitarians*. They believe that society ought to be strong. They say this is implausible, because each person's personality is made up by what they see in society. We can not have someone who can exist independently of society and say something is good or bad without it. The veil is flawed, because people only know what is good and just when they look at society. They need to know about the possibility of unfairness in society in order to make society fair.

Rawls said that these people behind the veil in the original

---

[49] In Ancient Greece, Aristotle considered the idea that like things should be treated alike and different things should be treated differently in proportion to their differences.

position should have a special way of reasoning: *reflective equilibrium*. Rawls said that people have many views that contradict. If you want to design society, you must find broad principles that explain these different viewpoints. It is not good enough to have multiple opinions: you must have structure which explains why you have these opinions. When you have that structure you have a principle of justice and how society should be run. Basically, Rawls says that his people in the *original position* have to sit there and try and think of principles which can reconcile all of their different viewpoints. This is what the courts have done in **Alcock.** Rawls says that you must come up with better principles: not just ones that come up with your political opinion, but core principles. So you take all of the examples/beliefs and try to find a general principle. Using this theory this is why the primary-secondary distinction should be maintained. However, what happens if this general principle does not work? It should then be weighed up and the principle which represents the largest number of the stuff that it agrees with, and get rid of the stuff that it does not agree with.

This process can be criticized. The problem is that we already start with court as an intuition which should not be part of the original position. We were told that the original position was about starting afresh behind the veil. If so, how can you have these different opinions about what is right and wrong? Another problem is that *reflective equilibrium* is difficult to do. How do you reconcile an excluding claim from rescuers over negligent defendants? How do you decide which is more important to you?

Problem Question

Christine has arranged a surprise hot-air balloon ride for her boyfriend, Mark. She joins the other spectators in the field and watches as the balloon, carrying Mark, Sam, who is the pilot, and three other passengers, takes off. Shortly after the balloon takes off, it catches fire and plummets to the ground. Horrified, the spectators run to the scene of the accident.

Mark and the other passengers have been injured in the accident. Sky Adventure Limited, the organisers of the event, have admitted liability in negligence for causing the fire and subsequent crash.
Advise the following, who have all been diagnosed as suffering from psychiatric injury, as to any legal rights they may have against Sky Adventure:

a) Christine, who saw the accident from the spectators field;
b) Sam, the pilot, who attempted to guide the balloon down safely;
c) Mark's mother, Jane, who heard of the accident on the local radio;
d) John, a policeman, who was driving past the field on his way home from work. He saw the burning balloon crash to the ground and went to try to assist.

Answer

Introduction

This is an advice for all been diagnosed as suffering from psychiatric injury, as to any legal rights they may have against Sky Adventure. First, this advice will discuss Christine, who saw the accident from the spectator's field. Second, it will advise Sam, the pilot, who attempted to guide the balloon down safely. Third. it will discuss Mark's mother, Jane, who heard of the accident on the local radio. Fourth, it will advise John, a policeman, who was driving past the field on his way home from work. He saw the burning balloon crash to the ground and went to try to assist. Lastly, this advice will conclude.

Restriction on Claims

The general principle for deciding if there is a duty of care in a case relating to negligently caused psychiatric injury is not straightforward. The courts in this area have adopted a different approach. The way they have done this is by imposing further conditions or criteria that must be satisfied before they are willing to accept a duty of care has arisen.[50] They do this by making a distinction between a primary and secondary victim. The difference between a primary and secondary victim was outlined by Lord Oliver in his concluding remarks in *Alcock v Chief Constable of South Yorkshire*[51] where he said primary victims are involved, *"either mediately or immediately, as a participant in the event created by the defendant's negligence'* and a *Secondary victim is 'simply a passive and unwilling witness of injury caused to others".*[52] It seems that the court tends to consider the 'floodgates' principle when trying to establish the

---

[50] Cooke, John. "Negligently caused psychiatric injury: A way forward?." Liverpool Law Review 17.2 (1995): 153-171.
[51] [1992] 1 A.C. 310
[52] [1992] 1 A.C. 310 at p.407

presence of a duty of care.[53] This suggests that imposing liability on the defendants could be overwhelming and needlessly burdensome.[54] Therefore the courts feel they must make it harder for secondary victim claimants to prove a duty of care.[55] This in turn is criticised as *"the area where the silliest rules now exist"*.[56]

Christine the spectator

Christine, saw the accident from the spectators field. This means Christine is a secondary victim. The case of ***McLoughlin v O'Brian***[57] established the criteria which assesses a secondary victim. Though it contradicts the extent to which the decision suggested was possible, the House of Lords however used the ***McLoughlin*** criteria, in ***Alcock***. The latter case is the principal case regarding secondary victims. The criteria used when considering whether a duty of care is owed includes:

1. Whether the Christine has suffered a recognised psychiatric illness;
2. Foreseeability of damage;
3. The relationship between the Christine and the victims;
4. proximity in time and space; and
5. The manner of perception.

First, it is vital to establish that Christine has a medical form of psychiatric illness. There will be no liability for distress,

---

[53] Teff, Harvey. "Liability for Psychiatric Illness: Advancing Cautiously." The Modern Law Review (1998): 849-859.

[54] Linde, Hans A. "Courts and Torts: Public Policy without Public Politics." *Val. UL Rev.* 28 (1993): 821.

[55] P R Handford, "Compensation for Psychiatric Injury: The Limits of Liability" (1995) 2 Psychiatry, Psychology and Law 37

[56] Dr J Stapleton, "In Restraint of Tort" in P Birks (ed), *The Frontiers of Liability* (1994) vol 2, pp 94-96

[57] [1983] 1 AC 410

fear or mental grief as a result of the negligence. [58] Thus Christine will have to provide expert medical evidence. Second, secondary victims must show actual psychiatric injury coupled with a reasonable foreseeability of physical injury.[59] Whilst it was foreseeable that Sky Adventure Limited might physically harm others with a negligent balloon ride, it was also foreseeable that anyone in Christine's position could suffer nervous shock as a result. Third, a duty will most likely exist where there is a close relationship.[60] Likewise, a duty will most likely not be present where the relationship between victim and spectator is remote. This is not restricted to relationships of blood; evidence must be provided regarding the closeness of the relationship. It is likely Christine will satisfy this criterion because Mark is her boyfriend. Fourth because Christine has been distanced from the scene of the accident this makes it difficult for her to justify recovery, because it will not be easy to establish foreseeability of the harm and it could be difficult to establish foreseeability of the claimant's harm. In **McLoughlin**, Lord Wilberforce submitted that the claimant must be at the scene of the accident, or be present at the accident's immediate aftermath.[61] As Christine was present at the accident in the spectator field, this will be enough to recover as she is in the aftermath. The last requirement is that Christine must have perceived the events with her own unassisted senses and as a direct consequence she suffered a psychiatric condition.[62] Christine will satisfy this requirement and her psychiatric injury is the product of "shock", because it caused a sudden assault on her nervous system.

Sam the pilot

Sam, the pilot, who attempted to guide the balloon down safely and as a result, has been diagnosed as suffering from

---

[58] **Hinz v Berry** [1970] 1 All ER 1074

[59] **Page v Smith** [1995] 2 All ER 736

[60] **Hambrook v Stokes Bros** [1925] 1 KB 141

[61] **McLoughlin v O'Brian** [1982] 2 All ER 298

[62] **Alcock v Chief Constable of South Yorkshire** [1992] 1 A.C. 310

psychiatric injury. Our starting point in this part of the advice is **Page v Smith**[63] where the House of Lords held a claimant had been *"directly involved in the accident" and "well within the range of foreseeable physical injury"*, then in this situation the claimant would be a "primary" rather than a "secondary" victim". This would mean a primary victim would be owed the same duty of care which applies in cases concerning physical harm. Lord Lloyd stated that it is vital for claims regarding psychiatric illness to make this classification. More recent cases have continued to make this classification.[64] Using the above authority we can advise Sam, that he was involved in the accident. He was at risk of dying if the plane crashed. Thus he will be regarded a primary victim and will be owed the same duty of care which applies in cases concerning physical harm by Sky Adventure Limited. Therefore, physical harm was foreseeable and thus Sam is likely to recover.

Jane hearing the accident on the local radio

Applying the *Alcock* rules to Mark and Jane, the risk of Mark's psychiatric injury was a reasonably foreseeable result of personal injury. Further, Mark and Jane are clearly close because they are in a mother and son relationship. However, Jane was not at the scene of the accident, and only learned of it by hearing about the accident on the radio. In *Alcock* it was held that claimants could not recover damages for nervous shock if they only saw the accident on television broadcasts, however the broadcasts did not even show the death of any person.[65] The same seems to apply in this case. Lord Ackner in *Alcock* submitted that certain situations where one sees a shocking accident on television broadcast, for example when

---

[63] [1996] A.C. 155

[64] ***Frost v Chief Constable of South Yorkshire Police*** [1997] 3 WLR 1194 at 1203; ***Hegarty v EE Caledonia Ltd*** [1997] 2 Lloyd's Rep 259 at 265-266

[65] Teff, H. "The Hillsborough Football Disaster and Claims for 'Nervous Shock'." Medicine, Science and the Law 32.3 (1992): 251-254.

a hot air balloon catches fire injuring the victims, could be successful on a claim for damages for nervous shock.[66] Nevertheless, this would most likely not apply in this case because Jane has not directly witnesses the catastrophe and would not be able to recover damages for nervous shock for Mark's injury.

John a policeman/rescuer

John, a policeman, who was driving past the field on his way home from work, when he saw the burning balloon crash to the ground and went to try to assist. We can begin by looking at the case of *Chadwick v British Railways Board* [67] where the claimant saw the consequences of a major crash situation while helping in the rescue of victims. He became psycho-neurotic as a result. In this case the claimant was actually a primary victim. The court placed the rescuer into the category of a "primary" victim discharging the control mechanisms. Waller J. said that it was foreseeable that *"somebody might try to rescue passengers and suffer injury in the process."* and *"shock was foreseeable and . . . rescue was foreseeable."*[68] Therefore it can be seen that the judge bases it solely on the foreseeability. Similarly in *Wigg v British Railways Board,*[69] the driver of the train attempted to rescue a victim who was trapped beneath the train and he was awarded compensation since he endangered himself and as a consequence of fearing for his safety, he suffered nervous shock. Tucker J. in *Wigg,* stated that foreseeability was only in question, citing Lord Bridge in *McLoughlin.*[70] In *Dooley v. Cammell Laird & Co Ltd*[71] load fell off as a result of a crane cable snapping. The operator of the crane believed that his colleagues below were injured thus suffering psychiatric injury. In **Galt v. British**

---

[66] [1992] 1 AC 310 at 405
[67] [1967] 1 WLR 912
[68] [1967] 1 WLR 912 at 921
[69] (1986) 136 NLJ 446
[70] [1983] 1 A.C. 410
[71] [1951] 1 Lloyd's L.R. 271

Railways Board [72] the claimant had heart problems as a result of the shock he suffered because whilst he was driving the train he nearly hit two men working by the lines. In both of these cases the courts felt it was right to make the defendants liable, thus throwing the claimant into a category of primary victim, with no mention to the control mechanisms, which were not invented during that period. Using these authorities it is likely that the court will place John into the class of primary victim on the grounds he is a rescuer.

There is an argument he was a policeman and under a duty to act thus an employee. In *White v Chief Constable of the South Yorkshire Police*[73] the claimants, who were police officers, helped remove dead bodies, carried those injured somewhere safe and resuscitated spectators in the Hillsborough football stadium disaster. They claimed as professional rescuers and employees for Post-Traumatic Stress Disorder resulting from their experiences. Their appeal was dismissed by the House of Lords. The Claimants argument can be summed up in Lord Goff dissenting comment:

> *"What rescuer ever thinks of his own safety? It seems to me that it would be a very artificial and unnecessary control, to say a rescuer can only recover if he was in fact in physical danger. A danger to which he probably never gave thought, and which in the event might not cause physical injury."*

The claimants relied on the abovementioned authorities of **Dooley;**[74] **Wiggs;**[75] and **Galt**[76]. Lord Hoffman dismissed these authorities on the basis they were *"ex tempore first instance judgments given on circuit."* For Lord Hoffman these

---

[72] [1983] 113 N.L.J. 870
[73] [1999] 2 A.C. 455
[74] [1951] 1 Lloyd's L.R. 271
[75] The Times, 4 February 1986
[76] [1983] 113 N.L.J. 870

decisions were regarded as cases raising questions of fact, more specifically if the plaintiff's psychiatric harm was foreseeable as a result of the negligent conduct of the defendant. This complied with the relevant law at the time (post *Alcock*). The House of Lords argued that the employee status of the claimant did not automatically place them from secondary victims to primary victims. **Alcock's** criteria for nervous shock applied. Although the claimants were professional rescuers, they were not exposed to any danger therefore this argument failed. Furthermore, the argument of their employee status failed too because it was held that an employee is not automatically a primary victim. Regarding the employer's implied contractual duty not to be harmed in the workplace, is no bigger than what is covered in tort law. The court felt that even though the police officers were entitled to sympathy, they were not entitled to anything more than others who witnessed this horrific event, such as doctors, and in this case especially grieving relatives which the law did not provide any compensation to. This analysis can be avoided and it can be argued that *White* will not apply to John because he is off duty and not under a contractual duty to help with no obligation. He placed himself in danger and becomes a primary victim as a rescuer.

Conclusion

Christine, who saw the disaster from the spectator's field, will satisfy all requirements of secondary victim and her psychiatric injury is the product of "shock", thus she can recover. Sam the pilot was at risk of dying if the plane crashed. Thus he will be regarded a primary victim and thus is likely to recover. Jane has not directly witnesses the catastrophe and would not be able to recover damages for nervous shock for Mark's injury. It is likely that the court will place John the policeman into the class of primary victim on the grounds he is a rescuer and he can recover losses for psychiatric injury.

Chapter 5 - Pure Economic Loss

Essay Question 1

Critically assess the development of liability for economic loss in negligence, using case law to illustrate your answer.

Answer

Introduction

> "Despite having the benefit of a series of decisions by the House of Lords on the subject of the accrual of a duty of care to prevent economic loss, the subject is far from being conclusively resolved."[77]

The law on the ability of the Claimant to claim compensation for economic loss has generated considerable debate. It is the aim of this paper to critically assess the law on liability for economic loss in negligence and its development by examining the relevant case-law. In order to achieve the aim of this paper, some of the authorities, both old and recent, relating to the subject matter at hand will be examined.

The Rules

Where the loss is characterised as a 'pure economic loss', that is, a loss where no damage has been sustained by the Claimant or to his property, the loss will be irrecoverable. Until 1991, the position was that in order to establish a duty of care in tort, the Claimant was only required to show whether or not a proximate relationship existed. He would then direct his mind as to whether there were any considerations which would suggest that such a duty should not be found.[78] According to

---

[77] Pigott, A., 'Economic loss, transmissible warranties and extensions to the boundaries of Murphy v Brentwood' [2005] *Construction Law Journal* 95 at p 95.

[78] *Anns v Merton London Borough Council* [1978] AC 728.

Pliener, this had *"the advantage of being (comparatively) straightforward and of applying the same principles for establishing a duty of care in relation to pure economic loss as to establishing a duty not to cause physical damage."*[79] Then came the seminal decision of the House of Lords in ***Murphy v Brentwood DC***[80] which overturned *Anns* and established the rule that a Defendant should not be held liable in the absence of a *"contractual or other relationship"*.[81] Four years later, Lord Browne-Wilkinson in ***White v Jones*** approved and followed *Murphy*, stating that:

> *"The law of England does not impose any general duty of care to avoid negligent misstatements or to avoid causing pure economic loss even if economic damage to the Plaintiff was foreseeable. However, such a duty of care will arise if there is a special relationship between the parties."*[82]

This had the effect of creating a two-system regime whereby two different tests operated independently of each other for pure and consequential economic losses. In order to succeed in his claim for pure economic loss a Claimant must now demonstrate to the court the existence of a 'special relationship'. According to ***Pigott*** there were only two categories recognised as giving rise to a 'special relationship': (1) where there was a fiduciary relationship[83]; and (2) where there had been a voluntary assumption of responsibility for economic loss.[84] It goes without saying that foreseeability must be shown if the Claimant is to succeed in his claim for pure economic loss, even if the court is satisfied that a special

---

[79] Pliener, D., 'Outflanking Murphy v Brentwood: claiming in tort for pure economic loss' [2010] *Construction Law Journal* 270 at p 271.

[80] *Murphy v Brentwood DC* [1991] AC 398.

[81] *Ibid* at p 489 *per* Lord Oliver.

[82] *White v Jones* [1995] AC 207 at p 274.

[83] See *Ross v Caunters* [1980] Ch. 297.

[84] *Hedley Byrne & Co Ltd v Heller & Partners Ltd* [1964] AC 465. See, *Pigott*, no 1 above, at p 99.

relationship between the two parties existed at the time of breach. The imposition of a duty of care upon the Defendant must also be reasonable for a court be persuaded to impose such a duty.[85]

There are other exceptions to the general rule that an action for negligence will only succeed where there has been a breach of a duty of care, either for personal injury to the Claimant or physical damage to his property but they are rarely accepted.[86] It must be noted that proprietary ownership is a necessary ingredient for a claim for the latter to succeed.[87]

Recent Developments

Pigott, in his study of two relatively recent first instance judgments, demonstrates how the confusing appellate decisions create uncertainty and injustice.[88] Depending on the trial judge's interpretation of the law, the Claimant is literally playing a gamble. In *Tesco Stores*[89] the Claimant Tesco brought an action against the Defendant Costain claiming that the Defendant was negligent in failing to provide appropriate fire stopping and inhibiting measures within the Store as constructed, and, second, that Costain was negligent in relation to the undertaking of an inspection of the Store in 1993 to assess the adequacy of the fire stopping and inhibiting measures in place and in reporting on the results of that inspection.[90] In giving his judgment, His Honour Judge Seymour Q.C. held:

---

[85] *Marc Rich and Co v Bishop Rock Ltd* [1994] 1 WLR 1071.

[86] See, *Junior Books v Veitchi* [1983] 1 AC 520 (defective items); *Ministry of Housing v Sharp* [1970] 2 QB 223 (breach of statutory duty); *Spring v Guardian Assurance plc* [1995] 2 AC 296 (references).

[87] See, *Leigh & Sillivan Ltd v Aliakmon Shipping Co Ltd (The Aliakmon)* [1986] AC 785.

[88] Pigott, no 1 above.

[89] *Tesco v Costain Construction Ltd* [2003] EWHC 1487 (TCC) (QBD (TCC)).

[90] *Ibid* at para. [13].

> *"...anyone who undertakes by contract to perform a service for another upon terms, express or implied, that the service will be performed with reasonable skill and care, owes a duty of care to like effect to the other contracting party or parties which extends to not causing economic loss".*[91]

In **Samuel Henry Payne**[92], on the other hand, His Honour Judge Humphrey Lloyd Q.C. differed and, following *Murphy*, opined that *"a designer is not liable in negligence to the client or to a subsequent purchaser for the cost of putting right a flaw in a design that the designer has produced that has not caused physical injury or damage".*[93] That was a case where the Claimants alleged negligence and breach of statutory duty regarding the advice given in relation to the construction and design of four cottages which were owned by the Claimants. After the properties had been sold it was discovered that the foundations for the buildings were not suitable for supporting the dwelling houses constructed and that substantial work was needed to remedy the defect.

Conclusion

The view advocated by **Pigott**[94] is adopted in its entirety. The *Tesco Stores* case is, as was suggested by the author, hard to justify bearing in mind the broad principle which is sought to establish. If the rule is adopted, it would almost completely erode the general rule laid down in *Murphy* and approved by courts over and over again that pure economic losses are irrecoverable for policy reasons, the most important being the floodgates argument. If the broad principle as enunciated in Tesco Stores is adopted, it would virtually mean that anyone

---

[91] *Ibid* at para. [230].

[92] *Samuel Henry Payne and others v John Setchell Ltd* [2002] B.L.R. 489 (QBD (TCC)).

[93] *Ibid* at para. [30].

[94] Pigott, above, at p 101.

who undertakes to perform services for another will owe a duty of care not to cause economic loss to the other. This is because it would not be long before courts implying that a person performing services ought to have exercised reasonable care and skill.

Essay Question 2

"The general economic torts are uncertain in their scope but perform a practical purpose, while the tort of conversion is certain in its scope but serves little practical purpose given the reluctance of the courts to extend the tort beyond application to tangible goods."

Is this a fair assessment?

Answer

Introduction

In this essay, the extent to which economic torts are certain in their scope and achieve a practical purpose will be examined. Subsequently, it will explore whether or not the tort of conversion is applied beyond tangible goods. Further, reasons for and against reform of the tort of conversion will be evaluated.

Economic Torts

The purpose of economic torts is to safeguard Claimants' interests[95]. Liability is a fundamental issue with economic interests; according to legal policy, [96] this is not an area of interests subject to protection under tort law.

Few legal systems permit competition to be unrestricted, despite the fact that it is deemed positively. What's more, it is maintained that "pure economic loss", which is unconnected

---

[95] Lewis, Richard. "The politics and economics of tort law: judicially imposed periodical payments of damages." The Modern Law Review 69.3 (2006): 418-442.
[96] Lord Millett explains the difference between legal policy and public policy in McFarlane v Tayside Health Board [2000]2 A.C.59 at 108 as the search for justice that accords with ordinary notions of what is fit and proper and the maintenance of coherence in the law

to physical damage, lies outside the parameters of tort law[97]. Economic activity is encouraged within a free economy by both public and legal policies; naturally some will profit whilst others suffer losses. The end result of the market is ultimately decided by the two factors of supply and demand. As Hobhouse LJ affirms:

> *"in a competitive economic society the conduct of one person is always liable to have economic consequences for another and, in principle economic activity does not have to have regard to the interests of others and is justifiable by the actor having regard to his interests alone."* [98]

This leads to the question, at what point a line should be drawn, and if so when it the responsibility of the law to intervene?

Tort law has faced difficulties in trying to find an answer to this question. Previously, rationalisation in terms of legal policy has proved problematic, and resultantly, tort law has manifested in to an intellectually and theoretically difficult area of legal practice, convoluted with inconsistency.

Policy considerations, regarding tort, have been influenced by ideas of just and fairness. However, notions of fairness are subjective to the individual, with many court cases tending to turn on technical points of law as opposed to addressing the issue actually at hand. The social context, in which the cases are decided, influences the decisions reached by the judges.

On the contrary, tort law has been keen to intercede with other areas, such as rights in intellectual property, reputation, tangible and intangible property, protection of personal liberty, security from physical injury.

---

[97] Rizzo, Mario J. "A theory of economic loss in the law of torts." The Journal of Legal Studies (1982): 281-310.
[98] Perrett v Collins [1999] PNLR 77 at 84.

In the 1898 decision of *Allen v Flood*[99], the majority within the House of Lords maintained that the Claimants did not have a legal right *"to pursue freely without hindrance, interruption or molestation the profession trade or calling that he has adopted for his livelihood"*.[100] At best, they possessed a freedom to pursue their professional occupation, *"conditioned by a precisely similar right in their fellow men"*[101] – meaning that, so long as others share the rights to act likewise, they may act as they wish in the pursuit of commerce– but in practice, how can this be applicable?

A commonality shared between all torts, is that they concern actions that are deemed to be beyond the norms of what is reasonable and fair.

Tort of Conversion

In the UK, conversion is a strict liability tort,[102] defined as a voluntary act by an individual that is inconsistent with the ownership rights of another.[103] For example, someone hauling lumber from a strip of land not belonging to him; a cohabitant removing common furniture from a dwelling and placing them in storage without the other cohabitant's knowledge or permission. As per Lord Justice *Diplock*, in *Marfani & Co Ltd v Midland Bank Ltd*:

> *"at common law, one's duty to one's neighbour who is the owner, or entitled to possession, of any goods is to refrain from doing any voluntary act in relation to his goods which is a usurpation of his proprietary or possessory rights in them. Subject to some exceptions…it matters not that the doer of the act of*

---

[99] Allen v Flood [1898] AC 1

[100] ibid

[101] ibid

[102] Kuwait Airways Corp. v. Iraq Airways Co. (No. 4,5,6) [2002] UKHL 19 [129]

[103] "[A] taking with the intent of exercising over the chattel an ownership inconsistent with the real owner's right of possession" (Rolfe B), Fouldes v. Willoughby (1841) 81 M & W 540, 550

usurpation did not know, and could not by the exercise of any reasonable care have known, of his neighbour's interest in the goods. The duty is absolute; he acts at his peril". [104]

The definition of intangible property is not widely agreed. However, we could describe it as a chose in action, since it can be characterized as "a personal right not reduced to possession". [105] However, the definition of "choses in action" includes a broad range of types, all with very different attributes and functions, whereas items of intangible property form a specific category, and share common characteristics [106]. "Intangible property" are all of those assets which are the subject of property rights. Intangible property is at the same time wider than choses in action as for instance patents are considered to be intangible property but not classed as choses in action. [107]

The English courts have considered whether intangible assets can be subject to conversion in OBG Ltd v Allan [108]. The House of Lords there ruled on several tort claims for financial loss caused by intentional acts. One of those entailed a claim for conversion concerning intangible property. The Defendants in this appeal were receivers who controlled the Claimant's assets and undertaking, in good faith. It resulted, however, that their appointment as receivers was procedurally invalid. As a consequence, the Claimants brought an action for trespass and conversion to land and chattels, for unlawful interference with contractual relations and for conversion of debts and contractual rights. The claim for conversion of debts

---

[104] [1968] 2 All ER 573

[105] "Conversion of choses in action" (1941) 10 Fordham Law Review 416 (Note principally prepared by Lester Rubin, member of the Board of Editors, 1940-1941).

[106] Sarah Green, The subject matter of conversion, J.B.L. 2010, 3, 218-242

[107] Attorney General of Hong Kong v Nai-keung (1988) 86 Cr. App. R. 174 PC (Hong Kong)

[108] [2007] UKHL 21

and contractual rights was a novel one and was not the main issue in the judgement, however its significance is great. This is due to the legal consequences of the judgment as well as to the extent of the damages claimed as the contractual claims amounted to 90% of the total assets.

The House was divided on whether intangible property could be subject of conversion. Lords Hoffmann, Walker and Brown refused to apply conversion to intangibles, while Lord Nicholls and Baroness Hale advocated for the extension of the tort to intangibles. The majority approach was outdated and maintains inconsistency within the law[109]. The distinction between tangibles and intangibles is great in regard to their physical form but not in regard to their legal characteristics.[110] Although, per Lord Brown at para 321[111], intangible property lacks the capacity of being possessed, and therefore is not covered by conversion. This approach depends upon a narrow reading of the definition of possession.

"… no less that the proposed severance of any link whatever between the tort of Conversion and the wrongful taking of physical possession of property (whether a chattel or a document) having a real and ascertainable value … to my mind there remains a logical distinction between the wrongful taking of a document of this character and the wrongful assertion of a right to a chose in action which properly belongs to someone else. One (the document) has a determinable value as at the date of its seizure. The other … does not."[112]

Evaluation of whether conversion should have been extended to intangible property

The House of Lords in that case had the opportunity to review the law and extent the application of the tort of conversion to

---

[109] S Green and J Randall, The fort of Cornw.1ion (Hart, 2009)
[110] OBG, [309-3 IOJ (Baroness Hale).
[111] OBG Ltd v Allan, [2007] UKHL 21
[112] ibid, para 321

intangible property. However, they declined to do so by crystallizing the application of conversion to tangible property only. The decision has sparked significant academic comment both in its favor and criticizing it.

In modern times there has been an increase in dematerialized assets, which are intangible in form. It has been argued that the law is not keeping up with technological developments and intangible assets are in need of protection. The economy would greatly suffer if digital commerce is discouraged by a lack of regulation. It has further been argued that in the modern electronic age, where intangible rights are held on behalf the actual owners without being evidenced in writing, the tort of conversion proves to be of great importance[113]. This part of the essay will assess arguments at both ends of the spectrum and evaluate whether the tort of conversion should be extended to apply to intangible property as well.

One of the arguments put forward for an extension of the tort of conversion arises from the fact that conversion has already been adapted to more modern forms of asset-holding such as cheques.[114] In fact, when intangible wealth is represented by a document, the court will award conversion damages beyond the mere value of the paper itself. This doctrine is know as the 'face value rule' by which conversion of a cheque will give raise damages equal to the amount represented by the cheque. "A document embodying or recording a debt or obligation should be treated as having the same value as the related debt or obligation".[115] It has been claimed that conversion by covering value-representing documents offers significant protection for intangible wealth. [116] This line of thought further argues that the courts should have gone a step further

---

[113] Green, Sarah, and John Randall. The Tort of Conversion. Bloomsbury Publishing, 2009.

[114] Goymour, Conversion of contractual rights, Lloyd's maritime and commercial law quarterly pp.67-91

[115] International Factors v. Rodriguez [I 979] QB 351, 358.

[116] Goymour, Conversion of contractual rights, Lloyd's maritime and commercial law quarterly pp.67-91

and allows the same protection to contractual rights lacking documentary manifestation. The argument is that the courts have already shown some willingness to adapt the tort of conversion to modern times with the doctrine of 'face value', however, simultaneously; they have also created more uncertainty in the law by creating a regime that leaves outside contractual rights. Therefore, they should extend conversion to all intangible rights to avoid complexities and confusion. As Lord Nicholls said as a matter of substance the law already protects certain contractual rights. It would therefore lack "rhyme and reason" not to extend the tort by analogy to pure contractual rights.[117] Another argument put forward for the extension of the tort of conversion to intangible property is that there has been a trend in the United Kingdom and abroad to give protection to intangible property as much as tangible property[118]. This is exemplified by the fact that in the United States the tort of conversion has already been applied to intangibles by the court[119]. Further, even in the United Kingdom, Parliament has recognized the necessity of protecting intangibles property by extending the application of the law of theft to them[120]. It has been argued that the court should follow this example by adopting a broader definition of 'possession' by, for instance, including excluding control over any type of assets, whether tangible or intangible.[121] On the contrary, very persuasive arguments have been put forward against an extension of the tort of conversion to intangible property. It has been argued that the language of the case-law on conversion is tailored narrowly only to apply to tangible property and would create confusion to try and apply language such as conversion by physical taking, by delivery, by wrongful but effective sale to intangible property.

---

[117] OBG Ltd v Allan, [2007] UKHL 21

[118] Goymour and Watterson, Testing the boundaries of conversion: accountholders, intangible property and economic harm, Lloyd's maritime and commercial law quarterly pp.204-226

[119] Kremen v Cohen (2003) 337 F 3d 1024

[120] S Green and J Randall, The fort of Cornw.1ion (Hart, 2009)

[121] S Green "To Have and to Hole!" Conversion and Intangible Property" (2008) 71 MLR 114

The rationale behind the language is that the property must be capable of being touched, taken or possessed. It is predictable that confusion and uncertainty will arise by trying to apply this language to, for instance contractual rights.[122] Perhaps, the most persuasive argument against the extension relates to the strict liability imposed in conversion torts. The defendant who interferes with the Claimant's chattel is liable at common law to repay its value despite lack of knowledge or reasonable belief that he was, in fact, acting wrongfully. The application of strict liability for conversion of intangibles could lead to very harsh results[123]. For example, a defendant who innocently took an invalid assignment of a debt from a person who had no proprietary title to the debt would risk not recovering from the debtor as well as finding himself liable in tort to the true owner of the debt assigned. Strict liability can lead to unjust results in some circumstances. In fact, Peter Cane, in Tort Law and Economic Interests (1991) at pp 28–29 stresses the interrelation between strict liability and tangible property:

> *"The 'logic' of these principles [of strict liability in respect of trespass to land and chattels] is that possession and the right to possess, being the core of the notion of property as it relates to land and chattels, deserve protection in their own right regardless of any fault on the part of the misappropriator. It is in this sense that the interest in possession is at the top of the hierarchy of legally protected interests: it is protected in itself and for its own sake."* [124]

Another persuasive argument against the extension of the tort

---

[122] Andrew Tettenborn, Liability for interfering with intangibles: invalidly-appointed receivers, conversion, and the economic torts, L.Q.R. 2006, 122 (Jan), 31-35

[123] Goymour and Watterson, Testing the boundaries of conversion: accountholders,
intangible property and economic harm, Lloyd's maritime and commercial law quarterly pp.204-226

[124] Cane, Peter. Tort law and economic interests. Oxford University Press, USA, 1991.

of conversion lies in the fact that other legal principles and doctrines afford protection to intangible property. For instance, the law of unjust enrichment covers most cases where the Defendant is enriched by the transfer from the Claimant's account. The situation is not so straightforward in other cases, however, it has been argued that it is still satisfactory. Where the Defendant is not enriched but still causes loss to the claimant or where the Claimant suffers greater losses compared to the Defendant's gains, there is no single applicable tort but 'unlawful means' or 'inducement' torts could be used. In the alternative, fault-based civil wrongs may cover those cases falling outside the specific torts. Therefore, one could argue that it is doubtful whether we need to extend the tort of conversion to deal with intangible property.[125]

Conclusion

This essay has argued briefly that general economic torts' application is uncertain in its scope as the court has not been able to draw a clear line between recoverable and non-recoverable damages due to the prevailing policy rationale that parties should be free to pursue their economic activities without too much legal interference.

The main body of this essay has dealt with the tort of conversion. The tort of conversion is indeed certain in its scope as its applicability is well established in case-law. One characteristic of this tort is that it has been held applicable to tangible goods only, with the limited exception of value-representing documents such as cheques. This essay has presented arguments both for and against the expansion of the tort of conversion to apply to intangible property. However, on the balance of those arguments, it would seem that the law as it stands provides enough protection to intangible property. It has been argued that the expansion of conversion would cause complexity and confusion due to its origin as a tort applicable to tangible property only. Further, the imposition

---

[125] Goymour and Watterson, Testing the boundaries of conversion: accountholders,
intangible property and economic harm, Lloyd's maritime and commercial law quarterly pp.204-226

of strict liability to conversion of intangible property could lead to very harsh results as liability would not be limited to those in a contractual relationship with each other. Finally, it has been argued by some commentators, that other existing torts or civil wrongs are appropriate and effective in the protection of intangible property, and therefore, the tort of conversion should not be extended beyond its current application.

Chapter 6 – Breach

Problem Question

Joe moved into a new flat last month. In an effort to save money, he asked his best friend Tim, a DIY enthusiast, to fit some shelves in his living room. Yesterday, the shelves collapsed, injuring Joe's head. It seemed that two of the screws had not been fitted properly.

Joe drove to the A & E department of his local hospital. In his dazed and concussed state, he nearly crashed into another car before running over Carolyn, a pedestrian, at a zebra crossing. When Joe was examined at the hospital, the A & E department was very busy and the doctor was eager to finish his shift. He failed to notice that Joe's range of focus was changing and that he seemed to have difficulty answering the doctor's questions. The doctor discharged Joe, telling him to rest. Joe was later rushed back to hospital where it was discovered he had an internal bleed in his brain. If this had been discovered earlier Joe would not have suffered the resulting brain damage.

Discuss any liability of Joe, Tim and the Doctor.

Answer

Introduction

This is an advice for all the parties concerned in relation to the events that have occurred. First, this paper will discuss Tim's liability to Joe for negligently fitting some shelves that have fallen and caused injury to Joe. Second, this paper will discuss Joe's liability for driving dazed and concussed state and running over Carolyn, a pedestrian, at a zebra crossing. Third, this paper will discuss the doctor's liability for failing to notice that Joe's internal bleeding in his brain that later resulted in brain damage.

The standard of care

This advice will be based on the law of tort and negligent conduct of Joe, Tim and the Doctor. Winfield said: *"Tortious liability arises from the breach of a duty primarily fixed by law: this duty is towards persons generally and its breach is redressible by an action for unliquidated damages."*[126] Thus in order for there to be an action of tort for each Joe, Tim and the Doctor, it will need to be shown that they owed a duty to the victim, i.e. that a duty of care was owed. It then needs to be determined if Joe, Tim and the Doctor's conduct fell below the standard of care that was required so that they have breached that duty.[127] Lastly it needs to be shown the existence of a causal link between the breach and damage caused.[128]

Tim's liability to Joe

Tim, a DIY enthusiast, agreed to fit some shelves in Joe's living room. The shelves collapsed, injuring Joe's head. It seemed that two of the screws had not been fitted properly. First it has to be established that Tim owed a duty of care to carry work out safely. In *Marc Rich & Co AG v Bishop Rock Marine Co Ltd (The Nicholas H)*[129] in which it was stated: *"... in order to determine the Defendant's liability in tort for negligence the court had to consider the elements of foreseeability and proximity and whether it was fair, just and reasonable to impose a duty of care on the Defendant..."*.[130] Assuming a duty of care is established then it must be shown that it was breached and conduct fell below the requisite standard.[131] The general principle is that the Defendant must

---

[126] Winfield in Rogers, W.V.H., *Winfield and Jolowicz on Tort*, 17th ed., 2006, p.5

[127] *Grubb on Principles of Medical Law*, 2nd edition, Oxford University Press, 2004

[128] Ibid.

[129] [1996] AC 211

[130] Horsey, Kirsty, and Erika Rackley. *Kidner's Casebook on Torts*. Oxford University Press, USA, 2015, p.67

[131] Charlesworth and Percy on Negligence, 11th edition, Sweet and

act as a reasonable person would in all circumstances. The definition of the reasonable man was provided by Alderson B in *Blyth v Birmingham Waterworks*[132] where he said:

> *"Negligence is the omission to do something which a reasonable man, guided upon those considerations which ordinarily regulate the conduct of human affairs, would do, or doing something which a prudent and reasonable man would not do."*

The assessment of what a reasonable man in the position of the Defendant would have done bases on an objective test, as stated in *Glasgow Corporation v Muir* [1943] AC 448. Therefore, when applying the reasonable man standard to Tim's conduct this must be done objectively and we must ask when Tim fitted the shelf and did not fit two of the screws properly, was this conduct reasonable, by normal standards. The answer is no. It is quite dangerous to fit shelves and leave the screws unsecure. Therefore, there was a breach of the duty of care. Nevertheless, Tim may try to argue that being an enthusiastic DIY does not make him a competent shelves builder. The fact that Joe was aware of his lack of expert competences, may be used to argue his liability. Nonetheless, the shelf collapsed, injuring Joe's head. Tim will likely be held liable to Joe for the injury sustained.

In respect of Joe's susceptibility to brain damage we are not sure it was caused by the shelf hitting his head, or late detection or of the two (discussed below). If Joe can prove the accident with the shelf was one Tim could reasonably foresee would cause injury, it will be irrelevant if the injury he sustained turned out to be greater than envisaged. In *Smith v Leech Brain & Co*[133] a Claimant suffered a small burn on the lip through a Defendant's negligence. This later became cancerous and the Claimant died as a result. The court held the tortfeasor "takes his victim as he finds him". It could also

---

Maxwell, 2006
[132] (1856) 11 Exch 781
[133] [1962] 2 QB 405

be argued the accident with the shelf made a "material contribution" similar to *McGhee v NCB*,[134] to Joe getting brain damage.

Joe's Liability to Carolyn

Joe drove to the A & E department of his local hospital. In his dazed and concussed state, he nearly crashed into another car before running over Carolyn, a pedestrian, at a zebra crossing. The facts here involve damage caused by Joe to Carolyn through a motor accident. It is well established and understood in law that a road user owes a duty of care to other road users.[135] In *Nettleship v Weston*[136] it was stated the driver should be judged by the standard of the ordinarily competent driver. If we apply this to our facts we can conclude Joe deciding to drive in a dazed and concussed state was a breach of duty owed to other road users. The fact Carolyn was also crossing on a zebra crossing as a road user Joe should have stopped on the road to give way to Carolyn. This is a further breach of duty as a road user. Therefore Joe will be liable to Carolyn for any injuries, pain loss and suffering she has sustained as a result of the accident. The breach of duty committed by Joe can also be showed by looking at the rule applied to Defendants under a disability. Whether the Defendant is aware or ought to have been aware to suffer of a disability that might affect the standard of care required, he cannot escape liability. This rule stems from the case of *Roberts v Ramsbottom* [1980] 1 WLR 823 in which the Defendant was a driver that unknowingly suffered from a stroke before taking his vehicle. He was unaware that he was unfit to drive but he realised that he was not well. Instead of stopping, he kept driving, colliding with the Claimant's car. The same ratio applied in this case by the court can well be used in the scenario. Joe was aware of not feeling well even if not conscious of the clinical reason of his state. Instead of stopping after the risk to collide with another car, he run over

---

[134] [1973] 1 WLR 1
[135] *Nettleship v Weston* [1971] 2 QB 691
[136] [1971] 2 QB 691

Carolyn. Even if Joe seems not morally blameworthy, his action will likely be still considered a breach of duty of care.

The Doctor's Liability

The doctor discharged Joe, telling him to rest. Joe was later rushed back to hospital where it was discovered he had an internal bleeding. When we consider the acts of a professional like a doctor, the courts will adopt a different test to determine the standard of care. The standard of care that is used is based on what the reasonable professional in that field would have done, rather than what the objective reasonable man would have done or achieved. An example of the standard that will be used was laid down in the case of *Bolam v Friern Hospital Management Committee*,[137] the liability of a doctor administering electro-convulsive therapy was considered by the court. The court said: *"A man need not possess the highest expert skill at the risk of being found negligent... it is sufficient if he exercises the ordinary skill of an ordinary competent man exercising that particular art."*

Professional negligence is a tort governed by rules of the common law of negligence. A doctor is supposed to attain the standard of a reasonably competent doctor.[138] The fact the A & E department was very busy and the doctor was eager to finish his shift and the doctor failed to notice that Joe's range of focus was changing and that he seemed to have difficulty answering the doctor's questions. The doctor discharging Joe, telling him to rest was potentially a breach of duty. If expert evidence is obtained that demonstrates the Doctor was wrong in discharging Joe and if evidence can be obtained to say that other tests should have been run by a responsible doctor in the same circumstances to determine the extent of his injuries, then the doctor will have fallen below the professional standard required and breached his duty. The difference

---

[137] [1957] 2 All ER 118

[138] Young, Andy. "Review: the legal duty of care for nurses and other health professionals." Journal of clinical nursing 18.22 (2009): 3071-3078.

between the standard of duty adopted by the doctor and, what other doctors in that art, may have done in the circumstances will be reviewed. The court will compare the Defendant's behaviour with the practice accepted as proper by a responsible body of doctors as per *Maynard v West Midlands Regional HA* [1984] 1 WLR 634. We are told that if detected earlier this could have prevented the resulting brain damage. Nevertheless, the Claimant must prove that the tortious act of the doctor has more than 50 per cent caused the damage. In Hotson v East Berkshire Health Authority [1987] AC 750, a child fell from a tree, breaking his hip. He went to the hospital but he did not receive the right diagnosis and went back home. Later on he developed a permanent disability. The ratio applied by the court based on the consideration whether the chance of recovery was less or more than 50 per cent. Therefore, if the doctor proves that the chance of recovery were in any case less than 50 per cent, his negligence does not satisfy the balance of probability test required to assess causation. On the contrary, whether there is breach of duty and likeliness more than 50 per cent to recover, the doctor will be held to have fallen below the requisite standard. The doctor and ultimately the hospital will likely be liable for pain loss and suffering of Joe.

Apportionment of liability

Both Tim and the Doctor are co-defendants in Joe's claim for damages for his brain damage. Tim may try and argue the subsequent worsening of his injuries i.e. late detection which lead to brain damage was too remote and not as a natural and direct consequence of his negligence. The question for the court is which losses can be treated as being caused by the original accident of the shelf falling on Joe's head and the late detection of the injury of internal bleeding.

In cases concerning 'multiple causes' as in this case, the potential causes of the brain damage suffered by Joe the court is faced with two possible causes here first the shelf falling causing internal bleeding and then the doctor negligently failing to detect the injury and treating it in time, *all of which are tortuous*. Thus the approach the court will take when dealing with causation is a more pragmatic one. This will be based on the court apportioning liability between the both the defendants in a way that produces a practical result and ensuring Joe has the compensation he needs to live with brain damage while recognising the respective fault of each defendant. In the case of *Fitzgerald v Lane & Patel*[139] the court established that whether there are two tortious actions coming together to cause the harm suffered by the Claimant, the court must apportion the damage between the Defendants. The trial judge held both Defendants liable as being at fault. It was not possible to say which collisions was the cause of the injuries. The judge held the two Defendants 1/3rd to blame. The Court of Appeal endorsed the trial judge's basic approach, but adjusted the proportions to the two Defendants 25 per cent each. Using this authority, the court may make Tim 30 per cent liable and the doctor 70 per cent liable to Joe to compensate him for his injuries. The difference in apportionment is to reflect their respective contribution to Joe's injuries.

---

[139] [1987] QB 781

Chapter 7 – Causation

Essay Question

"It has always been the law that a (claimant) succeeds if he can show that fault of the (defendant) caused or materially contributed to his injury. There may have been separate causes but it is enough if one of those causes arose from the fault of the (defendant). The (claimant) does not have to prove that this cause would of itself have been enough to cause him injury" (Lord Reid in McGhee V National Coal Board (1973)).

Discuss this statement.

Answer

Introduction

Firstly, this paper will explain the element of causation in relation to negligence claims and discuss the different tests produced by the courts to assess the presence of Causation i.e. material contribution/material increase in risk. Then, this paper will explain how to apply each test and conclude its findings.

Once the Claimant has proved the presence of a duty of care breached by the Defendant, the Claimant will have to show that the Defendant's breach has in fact and in law caused the damage. This is the element of causation that represents the nexus between the action of the Defendant and the injury suffered by the Claimant. In most cases, it is a simple application of the so-called 'but for' test that will establish causation. 'But for' the Defendant's action would the Claimant have suffered the loss or injury? Lord Hoffman stated extra judicially *"First, it is usually a condition of liability that not only should one have done, or been responsible for, some act which the law regards as wrongful, but that there should be a prescribed causal connection between that act and damage or injury for which one is held liable. There may be other conditions as well, such as that the harm should have been foreseeable. But some prescribed causal connection is usually required. Secondly, the question of what should count as a sufficient causal connection is a question of law...*" [140]

Once the breach is established, the Claimant must prove that it was the cause of the damage. This link or *'nexus'* between breach and damage is essential. Without it the Claimant's claim will fail, i.e. there will be no liability.

In order to determine whether there is the necessary link, two are the points that must be considered:

> 1. Factual Causation; and
> 2. Legal Causation.

Factual causation deals with establishing the actual physical link between the negligence and the damage/loss, whereas legal causation involves considering whether there are any grounds upon which the link should be regarded as having been broken. Factual causation represents the part of the analysis based on the 'but' for' test such as the Defendant's act or inaction (breach of duty) must be in fact the cause of the injury or loss suffered by the Claimant, as stated in **Cork v Kirby Maclean Ltd**.[141]

Nevertheless, the 'but for' test works inadequately in those circumstances where there is more than one cause to the injurious event. This is because it does not take into consideration each possible outcome. Injurious events can happen due to multiple causes. Multiple causes can also happen concurrently or in a consecutive way. According to the balance of probabilities test applied in relation to the 'but for' test, the Claimant needs to show that there is more than

---

[140] Lord Hoffman *[1] [2005] LQR 592 at 596-597*
[141] [1952] 2 All ER 402

50 per cent of probabilities that the Defendant's action has been the cause of the damage. Issues arise before multiple causes of the damage or whether there is more than one Defendant that caused the harm. The Court has developed different approaches to deal with these cases.

Material Contribution/material increase in risks test

In **Fitzgerald v Lane & Patel** [142], the Claimant was knocked down by the first Defendant when the lights were red for pedestrians to cross. He rolled of the bonnet of the car and was then run over by the second Defendant. It was established that both drivers had been negligent, but medical experts could not ascertain if injuries caused was the action of the first Defendant, the second Defendant or both. The issue was which one of the two and to which extent was liable. Since all drivers owe a duty of care towards the public and both of them breached that duty, the court awarded damage apportioned between the two Defendants: 25 per cent each and the rest 50 per cent was attributed to the Claimant as a result of his contributory negligence.

In those circumstances where there is more than one potential cause of the harm, equally plausible, the balance of probabilities test fails. In **Bonnington Castings v Wardlaw** [143], the Claimant contracted a lung condition due to the inhalation of dust. Inhalation was in some part a foreseeable consequence of his job. The rest was due to the absence of proper ventilation in the factory for which the employer was responsible. The approach adopted by the court in the circumstances was to assess whether the guilty dust caused by the negligence of the employer materially contributed to the disease. The answer of the court was yes.

---

[142] [1987] QB 781
[143] [1956]AC 613

Therefore, the Defendant was held liable.

This was followed in **McGhee v National Coal Board**[144] where the Claimant had contracted dermatitis. Again, the medical experts could not state with absolute certainty whether the dermatitis was caused by working in the kiln or through lack of washing facilities. The House of Lords found in favour of the Claimant on the basis that the Defendant had materially increased the risk of the claimant's injury.

In **Wilsher v Essex,**[145] the Court held that it was not enough for the Claimant to show that the Defendant's negligence caused the harm. It was required that the Claimant proved on a balance of probabilities analysis that the negligent action was more likely to have been the cause of the harm than the non-tortuous causes. In the case a prematurely born baby contracted an incurable eye condition that was the result of five potential causes. One of these was wrongful supply of oxygen in the blood. The doctor did this negligent mistake. Nevertheless, by applying the balance of probabilities test the court found that each cause amounted to 20 per cent of the source of the disease. Therefore, the tortious action of the doctor could have not been assessed as the main cause of the injury and the Defendant escaped liability. The House of Lords held that it was not enough for the Claimant to show that the Defendant's negligence could have caused the harm. The Claimant was required to prove, on a balance of probabilities test, that the negligent action was more likely to have been the cause than the other four potential non-tortious factors.

In **Hoston v East Berkshire Health Authority**[146] the Court adopted a different approach. A boy fell from a tree and broke his hip. He went to the hospital where he did not receive the right diagnosis. Years later he developed a permanent

---

[144] [1973] 1 WLR 1
[145] [1988] [1972] 1 WLR 1
[146] [1987] AC 750

disability. Medical evidence showed that there were 25 per cent of chances to avoid the disability, if the boy would have received the right diagnosis. The ratio adopted by the court in the case was the assessment of loss of chance. Whether the chance of recovery is less than 50 per cent, no compensation can be awarded.

Whether the Claimant's damage results from two or more consecutive events, the court has established that the second Defendant will not be liable for the original damage, as per **Performance Cars v Abraham**.[147] The Defendant negligently hit a car that was previously involved in a car accident. The court had to decide whether the two Defendants were jointly liable. In the absence of any additional damage to the original one already suffered, the Claimant cannot receive more compensation from the second Defendant.

In line with this approach, whether there are two tortious events and the second one does cause additional damage, the second Defendant will be responsible for his side of damage jointly with the original Defendant, as per **Baker v Willoughby**.[148]

It is now straightforward to conclude that the basic test will look at the presence of a link between the action of the Defendant and the harm suffered by the Claimant. Whether the cause of the harm results from different potential factors or more than one Defendant, the court will adopt the appropriate approach in the light of the circumstances of the case.

---

[147] [1962] 1 QB 33
[148] [1970] AC 467

Chapter 8 – Remoteness

Essay Question

How appropriate is the concept of foreseeability as the test for remoteness in the law of negligence? Discuss.

Answer

Introduction

The main topic of this paper is remoteness, the final element to prove in order to establish a claim in the tort of negligence. Once the link between the Defendant's negligent action and the damage suffered by the Claimant has been proved, the court will look at the extent to which the Defendant should be considered liable. Remoteness bases on a test of foreseeability. The issue is whether the element of foreseeability is appropriate in order to assess the level of liability of the Defendant. This paper will reach the conclusion of the significance of this element by looking at the relevant cases and the pertinent authorities.

Remoteness and Foreseeability

The question is whether the Defendant should be considered responsible for all the consequences arisen from his action. The law analyses the issue by looking at the likeliness or predictability of those consequences. Remoteness is a legal concept put into place in order to limit the potential liability of the tortfeasor (Elliot and Quinn, (2007), p104 et seq).

As Horsey and Rackley comment:

'When a court asks whether a harm was too 'remote' a consequence of the defendant's negligence (breach of duty), what is essentially being asked is whether the consequences of the negligent action were so far removed from it as to have

been unforeseeable by the defendant' (Horsey and Rackley, (2009), p247).

One of the first case that sets out a test to prove the element of remoteness is **Re Polemis** [1921] 3 KB 560, where the court tried to lay down a test to ascertain the element of remoteness. The facts involved a contractor company that was carrying repairs on a ship. In the attempt to load a cargo on the ship, a plank negligently fell into the hold of the ship. The spark, arisen from the fall, went in contact with petrol resulting in an explosion. The issue was whether the damage was too remote to be foreseeable. The court held that, even though it was not reasonably foreseeable that the spark could provoke an explosion, some damage the ship suffered were. According to the rule firstly established in this case, the Defendant was liable for all the direct consequences of his action. The court held immaterial that the explosion could not have been foreseen, since some damages were. The Defendant was held liable for all the direct consequences of his action.

However, **Re Polemis** was heavily criticised and the court took distance from its reasoning in the subsequent case of **The Wagon Magon (No 1)** [1961] AC 338 that has become the leading case on the matter. Here, the Defendant was carrying repairs out on his vessels at the Sidney harbour. Some furnace oil leaked into the sea. The oil spread reaching a close wharf, owed by the Claimant that was undertaking repairs on his ship. The oil set alight causing severe damage to the Claimant's wharf and to the Defendant's vessels. The court introduced the test of reasonable foreseeability, according to which the Defendant should only be held liable for an injury of the type reasonably foreseeable. The test bases on the concept of proportionality between fault and consequences. According to the court, it was not reasonably possible to predict that two days later the oil would have spread close to a ship where repairs were carried out resulting in fire and damages to the Claimant. The contamination damages caused by the oil were reasonably foreseeable, but that damage caused by fire was not to any reasonable person. Evidence showed that it was difficult to ignite such oil when floating on water. Damages were held too remote to consider the Defendant liable. Steele, (2007), p182 et seq).

The court moved on from the reasoning of **Re Polemis** by refusing the assumption that the Defendant is responsible for all the direct consequences of his negligence. Whether in **Re Polemis** the court attributed compensation for all damage resulting from the negligent action, in **The Wagon Mound (1)** case the court limited the concept of remoteness by looking at what a reasonable person may in fact have anticipated in the circumstances.

As Horsey and Rackley state:

"the question to be asked in order to establish whether the claimant's harm is too remote is this: 'Was the kind of damage suffered by the claimant reasonably foreseeable at the time the breach occurred?'" (Horsey and Rackley, (2009), p248).

The test established in **The Wagon Mound (1)** has become the sovereign principle of remoteness and it has been adopted in other cases, related to different fields such as actions involving the rule in **Rylands v Fletcher** [1868] LR 3 HL 330, as illustrated by decisions including **Cambridge Water v Eastern Counties Leather plc** [1994] 2 AC 264 and confirmed in House of Lords rulings including **Transco v Stockport Metropolitan Borough Council** [2004] 1 All ER 589, HL.

Just for the safe of completeness, it is important to mention that a second case called **The Wagon Mound (2)** [1967] 1 AC 617 led to a different judgment, even though it did not affect the general test established in **Wagon Mound (1)** in any substantive fashion.

Is Foreseeability the Right Test?

The discussion of this paper bases on the consideration of the appropriateness of the test of foreseeability to remoteness. At first sight it may seem tempting to argue against the test. The fact that the Defendant may be required to compensate all the consequences set in train by his negligent action may seem reasonable instead of allowing the escape of liability on the base that the consequences were not predictable. The limitation of the Defendant's liability on the basis of what was in fact reasonably foreseeable could appear morally not appropriate.

Viscount Simmonds mentions the concept of "current ideas of justice and morality" as the reasoning behind the assumption that individuals should be considered responsible for all the consequences of their actions. As Simmonds points out, the concepts of justice and morality do not contain opt-out clauses, exclusions or caveats so that foreseeability may seem to move from these higher concepts.

Nevertheless, Viscount Simmonds explained the reasoning behind the development of the law from **Re Polemis** to **The Wagon Mound (1)**. The purpose is to limit hitherto open-ended liability, which is justified. The incorporation of the foreseeability factor bases on the idea that it would be irresponsible to allow liability for all damages. This would lead to dangerous consequences that may affect the functioning of the whole society.

This point may be well explained by looking at the real world and insurability. It would be hard and expensive to acquire insurance for indeterminate and unforeseeable damages. The idea behind this example and what Viscount Simmonds is trying to prove is that the law must operate effectively and it cannot be based on abstracted concepts such as fundamental morality and justice. It has to be pragmatic and able to operate in the imperfect and complex world we live in.

The Wagon Mound (1)'s introduction of liability for foreseeable harms perfectly answers to the needs of the real world. An individual would feel restrained in undertaking activities, on which our society is in fact based, because intimidated by the risk of potential draconian and inestimable consequences of his actions. **The Wagon Mound (1)** test maintains liability for foreseeable harm, but at least prevents the imposition of liability for the unforeseeable (and possibly very far-reaching) consequences of negligent actions.

The case builds a balance between the need of the Claimant to see his rights restored and the importance to not impose inappropriate liability to the Defendant. The balance bases on the consideration of the form of damage suffered by the Claimant in the light of the facts. The circumstances of each specific case will be considered. This is also the reason why case law has illustrated that the courts have struggled to reach consistent decisions. It is understandable given the almost infinite range of possible damage-inflicting scenarios that the courts may be confronted with. In the case of **Doughty v Turner Manufacturing Co** [1964] 1 All ER 98 the court adopted a narrow definition of the concept of remoteness (here the distinction was between a splash and an eruption of burning liquid), while in **Hughes v Lord Advocate** [1963] AC 837 a more generous approach was adopted.

Concluding Comments

After looking at the reasoning behind the incorporation of foreseeability to the element of remoteness, it is now straightforward to conclude that this should remain the appropriate test to apply. 'If it is not broken, do not try to fix it', as the old fashioned common sense states. Viscount Simmonds' point of view in favour of the foreseeability element is proved and supported by its application to the real world. Furthermore, no better test has been set out yet that may justify a development from the current state of the law. The foreseeability test is far from perfect. Nevertheless, it is unreasonable to put it under discussion and criticisms as long as there is no superior alternative. Foreseeability perfectly answers to the need of a compromise between the two interests involved such as the Claimant's and the Defendant's. The test pragmatically answers to the need of recovery, but also to the possibility to undertake activities without limitless liability for any consequences.

When assessing the validity of a test in law, it is essential to look at its impact on the society and its conduct. It is not just the bare principle inherent in the test that counts, but also the influence it may exercise on the functioning of the whole society. Any test can be criticised and put under doubt on the basis of abstracted moral principles, but this would be deleterious. The application of the test of remoteness with a flexible approach in the light of the facts of each case is reasonable and encouraged. The test well protects the best interests of individuals and society in general.

In order to be appropriate a test must be able to answer to the vast majority of cases. It must serve the day-to-day interests of the whole society and not just the specific right on the single individual. The assessment of the validity of the test on the basis of its application in one single case is misleading. The test must be looked at by its general impact. As long as the test does not undermine the fundamental integrity of foreseeability as a good general benchmark of liability, the test must be held to be valid. It can be concluded that foreseeability test in remoteness represents the least imperfect measure of liability and the best compromise between the interests of the parties involved and those of the wider society that the law ultimately serves. Thus, on the basis of the foregoing analysis, Viscount Simmonds' contention is supported.

Chapter 9 – Defences

Problem question

On 25 January 2020, Britney left home at 6.30am to go for a run. She ran along the pavement on the main road going east out of Aberystwyth, starting from her home near Scholars pub.

After she reached the turn off for the industrial estate, there was no longer any pavement, so she ran along the edge of the road, on the right hand side facing any oncoming traffic. It was dark. It was raining. Britney was wearing dark grey running leggings and a bright orange running shirt but, because of the wet and cold weather, she also wore a black top over her running shirt.

About 100 metres further along, as she approached a bend in the road, a large truck, belonging to the Severn Internet Co and driven by its employee, came round the bend heading towards her. Another truck was approaching her from behind. Each took up nearly half of the road. At the last moment, the driver of the oncoming truck saw Britney but it was too late to avoid hitting her. Britney, who had been trying to get onto the grass verge, was hit by the side of the truck and suffered several broken bones.

Who is responsible for Britney's injuries?

Answer

Driver A owes a duty of care[149] is to all other road users (*Nettleship v Weston*[150]). We must first establish whether there is any primary liability of the driver A or rather his employers. Driver A, at the time of the accident was driving in the course of his employment and as he has committed a tort, his

---

[149] Road Traffic Act (RTA) 1988 and Highway Code
[150] [1971] 2 Q.B. 691

employers, may be liable under the principle of vicarious liability as the bus company was liable for the negligent act of its driver in *Limpus v London General Omnibus*[151].

Driver A approached a bend in the road, a large truck, came round the bend heading towards Britney. In *Glass v Donnelly*[152] there was similarly a bend in the road and the court held if the Defendant ("D") had been keeping a proper lookout, he would have seen the Claimant ("C"). Drivers must be extra vigilant and keeping a proper lookout on a bend, more so in the conditions and with oncoming vehicles, allowing for sufficient stopping time in all scenarios. Both drivers ought to be keeping a proper lookout for pedestrians to be present as in *Jackson v Murray* [153] and *Eagle v Chambers*[154]. Each lorry took up nearly half of the road. In *Eagle* Hale LJ in the Court of Appeal held when considering what just and equitable is must carry out comparative exercise being fair between the C and D. It was rare for a pedestrian to be found more responsible than a driver unless the pedestrian had suddenly moved into the path of an oncoming. It is arguable that both Lorries ought to have seen her and stopped in time for passing if keeping a proper lookout.

Driver A might be primarily liable because of a breach of the duty to take care. It may materialise he was driving too fast in dark wet conditions as he was unable to stop upon seeing Britney as in the case *Bruma v Hassan and Esure services Limited*.[155] We are told it was too late and Driver A could not avoid hitting her. In *Walker v Culina*[156] D was found not negligent and had braked appropriately when presented with the emergency. Britney has suffered damage in the form of pain and suffering because was hit by the side of the truck and

---

[151] Limpus v London General Omnibus Co (1862) Hurlstone and Norman 562 158 E.R. 993

[152] [2016] NIQB 36

[153] Jackson v Murray [2015] UKSC 5

[154] Eagle v Chambers [2003] EWCA Civ 1107

[155] Bruma (a protected party) v Hassan and Esure services Limited [2017] EWHC 3209 (Q.B.)

[156] Walker v Culina [2016] 11 WLUK 647

suffered several broken bones. _Eagle v Chambers_[157], places a high burden on drivers to reflect the vehicle they are driving is a potentially dangerous weapon, this generally continues to be the case.

The courts must also consider Britney's actions which may have contributed to the accident. We are told Britney reached the turn off where there was no longer any pavement. Moreover, she ran along the edge of the road. In _Walker v Culina Logistics Ltd_[158] C's claim failed because pedestrians were not expected in this area, there was no pavement and D had no reason to expect pedestrian, in grey clothing, might emerge to cross the dual carriageway on which his approaching lorry would have been manifestly visible for a considerable distance. Britney ran on the right-hand side facing any oncoming traffic. In _Belka v Prosperini_[159] it was held C was far more to blame than D, because he had suddenly moved into the path of D's oncoming vehicle. In Maria Sabir v Osei-Kwabena[160] it was said Pedestrians who step into the path of oncoming vehicles should attract a higher level of responsibility. In _Walker v Culina Logistics Ltd_[161] HHJ Charles Harris held C's own bizarre behaviour was the sole cause of his injury. Roaming in the dark across what he called "a motorway" in the face of a well-lit oncoming vehicle was an act of obvious and inexplicable folly.

Britney was wearing dark grey running leggings and a bright orange running shirt but, a black top over her running shirt. Although in _O'Driscoll v Bundred_[162] HHJ Sefton QC, dismissed contributory where a pedestrian failed to wear such clothing and risked the injury. Nevertheless the defence of _ex turpi causa_; prevents C's claim where their own actions were

---

[157] Eagle v Chambers _[2003] EWCA Civ 1107_
[158] (2016) Lawtel: Oxford CC – HHJ Charles Harris QC
[159] [2011] EWCA Civ 623 CA
[160] [2015]EWCA Civ 1213 CA
[161] (2016) Lawtel: Oxford CC
[162] [2019] 1 WLUK 646

blameworthy and accepting of the risk. Britney should have been wearing hi-visibility clothing. Her behaviour was the sole cause of his injury, running in the dark across unpaved road in the face of vehicles. Using the reasoning of the courts we can conclude that Britney has contributed by leaving the payment and she was bound to move into the path on an oncoming vehicle. Contributory negligence should be assessed at 50-70 per cent upwards *Froom v* Butcher.[163]

---

[163] [1976] 1 QB 286

Chapter 10 - Employers Liability & Vicarious Liability

Essay Question

The commission of an act that amounts to a criminal offence should never be deemed to be within the course of employment for the purposes of establishing vicarious liability. Critically discuss.

Answer

Since in law people are not responsible for the crimes of others, an employer or principal is not criminally liable for an offence committed by his employee or agent that he has not aided, abetted, counselled or procured, even though it is committed in the course of the employment or agency. This is because a central feature of the common law is that there is no liability for pure omissions. Assuming that the criminal is in full age and capacity, the law regards him as both morally responsible and legally accountable for his own actions and it seems pointless to hold some other persons (such as the employer) liable merely because he is richer or insured, also be regarded as legally liable for the crime. Such an action would not only make an employer liable for an omission for not preventing a crime, but it would also make him liable in cases where the law already holds the criminal himself liable.

Employers have thus argued that criminal acts like physical assault can never be seen unauthorised ways of carrying out authorised acts and should always be seen as acts committed outside the course of employment. Historical decisions have been inconsistent and many judges at many levels supported the above argument. However, in *Fennelly v. Connex South Eastern Ltd-and Vasey v. Surrey Free Inns Plc* (both cases concerning assaults on members of the public and both involving acts that were only marginally connected to the employee's actual job), this argument was rejected outright. Both concerned assaults on members of the public.

In *Vasey* the Claimant had kicked in a nightclub door and three doormen chased him a significant distance before beating him up. Stuart-Smith L.J stated "Not only was the attack so closely related in time and place for it to be a proper inference that they were reacting to the damage to the door… They were not pursuing their own purposes".

On the other hand, in **Fennelly**, a ticket inspector had inspected the Claimant's ticket but had continued a quarrel over his right to inspect the ticket. Objecting to being called an idiot, he followed the Claimant down the train where he assaulted him, placing him in a headlock. Buxton L.J. found that the ticket inspector was still in the course of his employment.

In **Lloyd v. Grace Smith & Co.** the House of Lords found a solicitors' firm liable for the fraud of a managing clerk on a client. The fact that the employee had acted for his own benefit was irrelevant. The decisive factor was that the client had been invited by the firm to deal with their managing clerk, who was therefore acting in the course of his employment. This decision established that it was not necessary for a Claimant to prove that the employee was acting for his employer's benefit.

Thus the above cases suggest that if the assault is work related, that is if it would not have arisen but for the employment context. Therefore, the employer would be held vicariously liable.

In relation to sexual abuse cases, the general rule was established in **Lister v Hesley Hall** where the House of Lords found the special school liable for the sexual assaults committed by its house warden. Traditionally the question asked in these cases is whether the tort complained of is a mode, albeit an improper and unauthorised mode, of doing what the employee has been employed to do. The Court of Appeal in *Lister* held that the sexual assaults were no such thing but rather were independent acts of self-gratification. The House of Lords, however, pointed out that the Defendants were responsible for the care of the vulnerable children and that the warden was employed to carry out that duty of care on their behalf. As Lord Hobhouse put it, this was a situation where the employers had assumed a particular relationship with the Claimants, imposing specific duties in tort on them and the employee was the person to whom they had entrusted the performance of those duties. The school was liable for the warden's acts because it was to him that the school had entrusted the performance of its duty.

In *Mattis v Pollock* [2003] the Court of Appeal held a nightclub owner vicariously liable for a stabbing committed by his doorman, notwithstanding he had specifically gone home to fetch a knife for the purpose. In *Gravil v Redruth RFC*, the Court of Appeal held the club liable for injuries caused by a punch thrown during a match by one of its semi-professional players.

Similarly, in *Weddall v Barchester Healthcare Ltd; Wallbank v Wallbank Fox Designs Ltd* [2012], the Court of Appeal has affirmed that, where an employee inflicts violence on another employee or third party, the vicarious liability of the employer for the employee's violent act will depend on the closeness of the violent act to the employee's employment.

Hence it appears that both physical and sexual assaults are capable of being considered unauthorised modes of carrying out an act of employment and the only relevant question is whether the acts were carried out in the 'course of employment', a phrase that is being interpreted more widely than before.

The doctrine of vicarious liability is a common law concept that is evolved by the courts to meet the changing needs and trends in society. Although the general rule adopted by courts is that an employer will not usually be liable for the criminal acts of employees, in special circumstances that is in cases where the closeness of the employment and the criminal offence makes it fair, just and reasonable to impose such a vicarious liability. Therefore, in certain situations criminal offences should be deemed to be within the course of employment if such a conclusion is necessary for policy reasons (as identified by the Canadian Supreme Court in ***Bazley v Curry***), like (a) imposing vicarious liability encourages the employer to be careful in the selection and supervision of his workforce; (b) the employer is better able to compensate the Claimant; (c) the employer who stands to benefit from the enterprise on which his ex-hypothesis tortious employee was engaged should according accept the burden and compensate the victim for the resulting loss.

Chapter 11 - Occupiers Liability

Problem Question

Ahmed went to do his shopping at Fastmart Ltd early one winter's morning. He slipped on the icy path up to the entrance, and fractured his wrist. Fastmart Ltd has said that it was the responsibility of Wipeit Ltd, who are cleaning contractors employed by Fastmart Ltd.

John, an electrician, was contacted by Fastmart Ltd, and asked to fix a faulty light switch in the stockroom. While he was doing the work, he suffered a massive electric shock from a loose wire, and was killed.

Fastmart Ltd's car park has been used recently by youths to play football. Fastmart Ltd has erected a sign at the entrance to the car park saying "This car park is strictly for the use of customers only." Wally, aged seventeen, and his friends ignored the sign and were playing football when the ball was kicked onto the flat roof of the shop. Wally offered to climb up to retrieve it. He fell through the roof and suffered head injuries.

Advise Fastmart Ltd as to their liability to Ahmed, John's next of kin and Wally, if any.

Answer

Introduction

First, this paper will advise Fastmart Ltd as to their liability to Ahmed, who slipped on the icy path up to the entrance. Second, this paper will advise John's next of kin, if they can recover any compensation for John death. Lastly this paper will advise Fastmart as to their liability to Wally, who has fallen through their roof and suffered head injuries.

Liability to Ahmed

Ahmed slipped on the icy path up to the entrance, and fractured his wrist. Fastmart Ltd has said that it was the responsibility of Wipeit Ltd, who are cleaning contractors employed by Fastmart Ltd. Section 2(4)(b) Occupier Liabilities Act 1957 states:

"where damage is caused to a visitor by a danger due to the faulty execution of any work of construction, maintenance or repair by an independent contractor employed by the occupier, the occupier is not to be treated without more as answerable for the danger if in all the circumstances he had acted reasonably in entrusting the work to an independent contractor and had taken such steps (if any) as he reasonably ought in order to satisfy himself that the contractor was competent and that the work had been properly done."

Thus Fastmart will not be liable if they can show they entrusted the work to Wipet Ltd a suitably qualified professional firm in order to clear the icy path at the entrance. In *Haseldine v Daw* [1941] 2 KB 343 a lift in a block of flats fell and crashed at the bottom and killed a person. The contractors were competent in the past and nature of their work was specialist in nature and it was not reasonable to expect the landlord, as occupier, to inspect the quality of that work. However, it can be argued Fastmart Ltd could have seen the entrance had an icy path and could have told Wipeit Ltd to have done something about it. In *Woodward v Mayor of Hastings* [1945] KB 174 a child was injured by a snow covered step. All could have been seen was that the step was not swept clean from snow. The occupier should have checked the step was cleaned.

Liability to John

Section 2(3) Occupier Liabilities Act 1957 states:

"The circumstances relevant for the present purpose include the degree of care, and want of care, which would ordinarily be looked for in such a visitor, so that (for example) in proper cases:... (b) An occupier may expect that a person, in the exercise of his calling, will appreciate and guard against any special risks ordinarily incident to it, so far as the occupier leaves him free to do so."

Therefore, persons with specialist skills, such as John since he is an electrician, who is familiar with working in potentially hazardous environments, will be expected to have some regard for his own safety and Fastmart will not be automatically liable for any mishap. In *Roles v Nathan* [1963] 2 All ER 908, the owner of a coke-fired boiler called in two chimney sweeps to seal a sweep hole in the flue. He warned them there might be gas fumes, and he gave a general warning that the boiler was not to be used again until the sweep hole was sealed. The sweeps tried to seal the flue while the boiler was still in use, and died from the fumes. The Court of Appeal dismissed the claim by the sweeps' families: the sweeps were exercising their profession and should have been aware of the particular dangers. In *General Cleaning Contractors v. Christmas* [1953] AC 180, a window cleaner was balancing awkwardly and was injured. This was a risk of the window cleaner should be aware of. He was however able to sue his employers for not operating a safe system of work.

Liability to Wally

Wally, aged seventeen, and his friends ignored the sign and were playing football when the ball was kicked onto the flat roof of the shop. Wally offered to climb up to retrieve it. He fell through the roof and suffered head injuries. Wally is a trespasser. The Occupiers Liability Act 1984 covers all those on premises other than lawful visitors - mainly trespassers. But the duty it imposes on the occupier, is like the "duty of common humanity", is limited to dangers of death and personal injury.

The first question in considering possible liability under the 1984 Act is whether in the particular circumstances the occupier had a duty of care at all. Such a duty is not automatic, and arises only where the conditions set out in Section 1(3) is fulfilled. An occupier of premises owes a duty to another (not being his visitor) in respect of any such risk referred to in subsection (1) if –

(a) He is aware of the danger or has reasonable grounds to believe it exists;

(b) He knows or has reasonable grounds to believe that the other is in the vicinity of the danger concerned or that he may come into the vicinity of the danger (in either case whether the other has lawful authority for being in that vicinity or not); and

(c) The risk is one against which, in all the circumstances of the case, he may reasonably be expected to offer the other some protection.

Once a duty has been established according to the criteria set out in Section 1(4), above, it is incumbent upon Fastmart *'to take such care as is reasonable in all the circumstances of the case to see that he does not suffer injury on the premises by reason of the danger concerned'*. In determining what is reasonable, the courts must balance the magnitude of the risk against the burden which removing the risk would place on the occupier. In *Vodden v Gayton* [2001] PIQR 4, a person was exercising a right of way, a rutted farm track on a moped. He fell off and got injured. It was unreasonable to expect the farm owner to fill in all the ruts and potholes for a moped driver.

The Warning

Fastmart Ltd has erected a sign at the entrance of the car park saying "This car park is strictly for the use of customers only." Taking steps to warn potential trespassers of the danger may discharge the duty, as established in Section 1(5), although there is no duty to warn against obvious dangers. In *Ratcliff v McConnell* [1999] 1 WLR 670, a 19-year-old student climbed over a locked gate late one night and dived into the swimming pool (which was closed for the winter and partially drained). He apparently dived into the shallow end, and hit his head on the bottom, causing injuries, which left him almost totally paralysed. He sued the College under the Occupier's Liability Act 1984 and the trial judge found in the students favour subject to a deduction for contributory negligence. Allowing the appeal, Stuart-Smith LJ said there were several warning notices around the pool, and the dangers of diving into water of unknown depth were too well-known to need any further express warning. The student had accepted the risks, and under Section 6 of the Act his claim must fail.

Chapter 12 - Trespass, Nuisance, Rylands v Fletcher

Problem Question

Rave, the owner of a suburban house, converted an existing barn in the grounds of the property into a music studio. Rave then let the entire property on a ten year lease to Trend, who allowed various local rock groups to use the studio free of charge for practice. Noise from this activity caused considerable annoyance to the young daughters of Square, who owned and lived in the house next door, though not to Square himself, since he was completely deaf.

Fans of one of the groups besieged the studio, leaving large quantities of rubbish in the garden; this attracted mice and rats, which soon infested the basement of Square's house.

Vibrations from the music dislodged loose slates from the barn roof; these fell into Square's garden, injuring one of his daughters and breaking several panes of glass in his greenhouse.

Analyse the rights and liabilities of all the parties.

Answer

Introduction

This is an advice for all the rights and liabilities of all the parties. This advice will, firstly, discuss the noise from the activities of the studio. Secondly, the advice will discuss the large quantities of rubbish which has attracted mice and rats. The third point will be the consideration of the vibrations from the music which dislodged loose slates.

The Tort of Nuisance

Private nuisance has been defined as: *"...any continuous activity or state of affairs causing a substantial an unreasonable interference with a plaintiff's land or his use or enjoyment of that land."*[164] Any activity, which interferes with the use and enjoyment of a neighbour's property, is a potential nuisance. Whether an activity is a nuisance is a matter to be determined by the court.

The Noise

Noise from this activity caused considerable annoyance to the young daughters of Square. Square was not disturbed himself, since he was completely deaf. This poses a problem here because nuisance is a tort to land, hence only those with a sufficient proprietary interest in land have standing (*locus standi*) to seek a remedy. For example, in **Malone v. Laskey**[165] the injured wife of a manager of business premises (who occupied the premises under a licence of his employers) could not claim as she had no sufficient proprietary interest in land. Hence, if the two daughters decide to bring a claim, their claim against the owner and inhabitants of suburban house music studio will fail because they do not have a propriety interest in the land.

The Rats and Mice

Fans of one of the groups besieged the studio, leaving large quantities of rubbish in the garden; this attracted mice and rats, which soon infested the basement of Square's house. Here the issue of a propriety interest will not pose a problem. Square is the land owner and may bring an action.

Who is responsible?

However, the concern here is against whom Square should bring the claim against. Fans of one of the groups that have

---

[164] **Bamford v Turnley (1862) 3 B & S 66**
[165] [1907] 2 KB 141

besieged the studio are responsible. The usual Defendant is the occupier of the land from where the nuisance has come. He can be liable for nuisances created by himself as well as those created by others. The occupier's responsibility derives from the fact that he has control over the land and occurrences upon it.[166][167] It may well be that the fans are trespassers. The inhabitants of suburban house music studio (occupier) will not normally be liable for nuisances caused by trespassers. Here the inhabitants of the music studio will again only be liable, if they have continued or adopted the nuisance.[168] However, the occupier may escape liability if he shows to have taken reasonable steps to abate the nuisance.

Indirect Interference

In order for Square to bring a successful challenge, he must further show the nuisance was an indirect interference, damage was caused and this was an unlawful interference with his land. Thus first private nuisance concerns indirect interference with the use or enjoyment of the Claimant's land in contrast with direct interference, which would be trespass. What amounts to indirect interference is governed by the principles laid down by the courts. Sounds, smells and vibrations have all been held to be indirect interference. In **Sedleigh-Denfield v O'Callaghan** a flood of water was held to be capable of constituting a private nuisance. The rats and mice would certainly be an indirect interference. However, there may also arguably be a possible claim under the rule from **Rylands v Fletcher**[169] *that allows* the Claimant to bring a claim for damage suffered due to something the Defendant has brought on his land and which has escaped.

Damage

---

[166] **Leakey v National Trust** [1980] 1 All ER 17
[167] Bermingham & Brennan, Tort Law, 2nd Ed., 2010, (Oxford: OUP), at p. 232
[168] As illustrated in **Sedleigh-Denfield v O'Callaghan** [1940] AC 880; also Bermingham and Brennan at page 236
[169] [1868] UKHL 1

Private nuisance is not actionable *per se* as the Claimant must establish that he has suffered some damage. In **St Helens Smelting v. Tipping**[170] the Claimant bought an estate near a smelting works, and then complained that the fumes were damaging his trees and other crops. This was physical damage to his property, and his claim succeeded. Therefore, as there is a presence of rats and vermin on the land this will be seen as damage by the courts as pet control will have to be called out to remove the infestation of rats and mice from Square's cellar.

Unlawful Interference

As stated above, Stamp must show that the nuisance he is complaining of constitutes *'unlawful interference with his enjoyment or use of the land'.*[171] The term 'unlawful' in this context denotes unreasonableness rather than illegality. The question that the courts will look at is not whether the Defendant is at fault in any way, but whether the activity, that is causing the nuisance, can be said to be reasonable use of his land. The courts will do this by looking at the following: character of a neighbourhood or 'locality'; utility/public benefit; time and duration; continuing state of affairs; abnormal sensitivity and malice (the last two being irrelevant to Stamp's case).

Locality

The courts when looking at neighbourhood or 'locality' may find that the location of the recording studio is not suitable for a suburban house. However, in **St Helens Smelting v Tipping**[172] Lord Westburry added an important proviso if physical damage has actually occurred then that can never be reasonable.

---

[170] (1865) 11 HLC 642
[171] **Bamford v Turnley** (1862) 3 B & S 66
[172] (1865) 11 HLC 642

Public Benefit

If the Defendant's activities serve a useful purpose or benefit to the community, this will not mean that the Defendant has not committed a nuisance. In **Adams v Ursell**[173] the court recognised that there was a public benefit in the Defendant's fish and chip shop. This consideration was, however, outweighed by the nature of the area where the shop was operating, and the interference with the Claimant's use of land. The studio provides a benefit of bringing affluence to the area but this will be outweighed by the nuisance it is causing.

Duration

In **Kennaway v Thompson**,[174] it was stated that it will be important to see when the alleged nuisance takes place, how long it continues and how frequently it is repeated. Whether the act does constitute a nuisance here will be determined by reference to all the circumstances of the particular case *"... the time of commission ... the place of commission ... the manner of committing it ..."*.[175] The court is likely to view this as nuisance.

Continuing state of affairs

It will be necessary to show that the nuisance arises from a continuing state of affairs. There will not usually be liability in private nuisance for an isolated incident. In such instances claims may have to be brought in negligence or, if it is possible, by means of an action under the rule in **Rylands v Fletcher**. However, it may be that a single incident could be a nuisance, if it illustrates an underlying state of affairs, as in Spicer v Smee[176] where a fire started in a bungalow that had

---

[173] [1913] 1 Ch 269
[174] [1981] QB 88
[175] **Stone v Bolton** [1949] 1 All ER 237 at 238-9 Oliver J)
[176] [1946] 1 All ER 489

defective wiring. Although the fire was an isolated incident, the defective wiring which had continued for some time amounted to a dangerous underlying state of affairs. The same could be argued here that the rubbish constituted a dangerous underlying state of affairs.

Rylands v Fletcher

The case of Rylands v Fletcher[177] gave rise to a principle which confers a right of action on a Claimant who has been damaged by something which the Defendant has brought on to his land it has been an non-natural use of that land[178] and which has escaped.[179] The case was originally based in nuisance but over the years has developed a status of its own. It is now regarded as a separate rule in tort law imposing strict liability where an isolated escape had occurred. It can be argued in this case there has been an escape of rubbish on the land and this being dropped by the fans has been a non-natural use of the land (which caused the infestation). However, the rule's practical usefulness is limited and successful actions are relatively rare. There have been no successful cases since World War II. The House of Lords were invited to dismiss the Rylands rule in **Transco plc v Stockport MBC**[180] but declined to do so. It was felt that such an action would leave a lacuna in the law.

The Vibrations

Square can bring an action for this nuisance because to reiterate he is the land owner. The vibrations are an indirect interference. Damage has been caused because slates have injured one of his daughters and broken several panes of glass in his greenhouse. This will be deemed an unlawful interference because of the principle in **St Helens Smelting v.**

---

[177] (1868) LR 3 HL 330
[178] **Smeaton v. Ilford Corporation** [1954] 1 All ER 293
[179] **Rigby v. Chief Constable of Northants** [1985] 2 All ER 985
[180] [2004] UKHL 61

Tipping,[181] where Lord Westburry added an important proviso if physical damage has actually occurred then that can never be reasonable. One possible partial defence that could be run by the studio is Square's slates were loose and that a reduction be made from any damages awarded for contributory negligence. [182]

---

[181] (1865) 11 HLC 642
[182] s1 Law Reform (Contributory Negligence) Act 1945

Chapter 13 - Defamation

Essay Question

The protection of individual's from defamation is just as important as the protection of the press's freedom of expression. Discuss.

Answer

This paper will make a case for the repealing various defamation laws in relation to journalists. This change will be advocated because it sits uneasily with Article 10 of the European Convention on Human Rights ("ECHR") (as implemented into English Law through the Hum Rights Act 1998). This paper will argue that this although not stature law but rather common law should be repealed to prevent journalists being subject to the view that their right to freedom of expression preserved within Article 10 of the ECHR is at risk every time they produce a piece of work, the contents of which may lead to a finding of libel by defamation.[183]

What is the right preserved in Article 10, one may ask? Article 10 states that *"(1) Everyone has the right to freedom of expression. This right shall include freedom to hold opinions and to receive and impart information and ideas without interference by public authority and regardless of frontiers"* At present journalists whether newspaper or on television or radio, are subject to the provisions of Section 166 of the Broadcasting Act 1990. This legislation provides that the publication of defamatory words, pictures, gestures and other statements amounts to libel.[184] Steele defines defamation with reference to Lord Atkin's judgement in *Sim v Stretch*[185] as

---

[183] M, Jones, "Textbook on Torts" (Blackstone Press Limited, 2000) Page 495

[184] T, Weir, "A casebook on Tort" (London, Sweet & Maxwell, 2004) page 520

[185] [1936] 2 All ER 1237

"exposing the plaintiff to hatred, ridicule and contempt" and lowering the planitiff in the estimation of right-thinking members of society generally.[186]

Arguably journalists play a crucial part in society by holding particularly individuals in power[187] to account as argued by J G Flemming in his book.[188] If they continue to be restrained in doing so by anti-defamation legislation, this arguably limits the extent of the important job that they do. This papers issue with the current legislation on defamation and regarding section 2 of the Defamation Act 1952, is that there is no requirement to prove special damage to show that Defamation has occurred.

This papers interpretation of this is that a journalist would not have to necessarily cause damage to an individual's reputation, when they have spoken against them on television or radio, the possibility that the words that they have used would be enough to render them liable for an action in defamation. Arguably despite the attempts in cases such as *Lewis v. Daily Telegraph*[189] to introduce some common sense into whether journalists should be held liable for what amount to be truthful statements, earlier cases such as *Hough v London Express*[190] serve to show that as regards innuendo, the person knowing the relevant facts does not need to understand the article to contain defamatory material.[191]

Despite my central rationale being that the legislation regarding defamation should be repealed, there have been

---

[186] as J, Steel, "Tort Law: Text, Case and Materials" (Oxford University Press, 2007) page 761

[187] F, Trindade, "Defamatory Statements and Political Discusssion" (2000) 116 LQR 185, K, Williams, "Defaming Politicians: The not so Common Law" (2003) 63 MLR 748

[188] J, Fleming, "The Law of Torts (9th Edition, NSW: Law Book Company, 1998) Page 648

[189] [1964] AC 234

[190] [1940] 2 KB 507

[191] J, Steele *op cit* page 766

attempts in case law to provide some defence for journalists, and in relation to preserving journalists' freedom of expression.[192] The fair comment defence clarified by Lord Denning in **Slim v Daily Telegraph**[193] was of particular significance summed as *"the right of fair comment is one of the essential elements which go to make up our freedom of speech. We must ever retain this right intact. It must not be whittled down by legal refinements"*.[194]

Furthermore, LJ Scott in **Lyon v Daily Telegraph** [195]clarified that *"The reason why, once a pleas of fair comment is established, there is no libel is that it is in the public interest to have a free discussion of matters of public interest."* There was a similar finding in **Cheng v Tse Wai Chun Paul**[196] , and in **Reynolds v Times Newspapers Limited**,[197] by Lord Denning. Moreover, in by Lord Porter in **London Artists v Littler**,[198] in **Kemsley v Foot**,[199] in **Rupert Lowe v Associated Newspapers**[200], in **Telnikoff v Matusevitch**[201] and in **Branson v Bower**.[202]

The fact that there has been so much case law on this is welcome, but also significant. The reason for the proliferation of case law is that the courts have sought to fill the gap in the law relating to defamation to describe and define fully, why arguably there is no specific reference to the human rights of journalist in the existing legislation to express their views

---

[192] (see also in relation to confidential information, page 1004 L, Bently and B, Sherman, "Intellectual Property law" (Oxford University Press, 2009) page 1002
[193] [1968] 2 QB 157
[194] E, Barendt, "Libel and Freedom of Speech in English Law [1993] PL 449
[195] [1943] KB 746
[196] [2000] 4 HKC 1 at page 14
[197] [2001] 2 AC 127
[198] [1969] 2 QB 375
[199] [1952] AC 345
[200] [2006] EWHC 320
[201] [1992] 2 AC 343
[202] [2002] QB 737

freely in pursuance of Article 10 of the European Convention on Human Rights.[203] The reason for the lack of specific defamation legislation to support the human rights of journalists maybe that the legislators have come to the view that the imposition of Article 10 of the European Convention of Human Rights into UK law by section 3 of the Human Rights Act 1998, was sufficient to impose also the right to freedom of expression for journalists.

However arguably this paper submits this was insufficient as although Article 10 protects journalists' right to freedom of speech, it also restricts this right in relation to defamation. Article 10(2) of the ECHR state that *"the exercise of these freedoms, since it carries with it duties and responsibilities may be subject to such formalities, conditions, restrictions or penalties as are prescribed by law and are necessary in a democratic society .... For the protection of the reputation or rights or others."* This reference to reputation is very important. This papers proposal for the repeal of the law relating to defamation as regards journalists, is that all the work of journalists should be free of an action in defamation. Yes arguably this is a very radical proposal however, my view is that journalists should be trusted and expected to use their professional judgment in embarking on their work. No doubt with this trust comes a great deal of responsibility. One proposal to curb journalists and the statements they make could be more professional conduct of journalists, such as a code of practice. However in its absence, depending on the view or rationale in a court under the current system if a journalist is faced with defamation proceedings, journalists run the risk of being found guilty of defamation, when they are merely performing their important role in society.

Further particularly in relation to publication or broadcasting as regards criminal prosecution the European Court of Human Rights is driven to draw an interference as occurred in cases

---

[203] Richardson & Thomas, "Archbold 2003" (Thomson Sweet & Maxwell) page 1544.

such as ***Handyside v UK, X Ltd v UK***[204] ***Lingens v Austria***[205], **Muller *v Switzerland,***[206] ***Jersild v Denmark,***[207] ***Otto-Premiger-Institut v Austria,***[208] ***Prager and Obershclick v Austria***[209]** and the UK case of ***Goodwin v UK***[210][211] that it contravenes the right to freedom of expression. This papers Argument is that if a criminal prosecution relation to defamation mounts a challenge to freedom of expression a civil claim against journalist should also be deemed to be in contravention of journalists' right to free speech.

However the justification for my central thesis that the defamation legislation needs to be repealed in relation to journalists is best summed up by Lord Diplock in the 1980 case of ***Gleaves v Deakin***[212] in which he said that the "English offence of defamatory libel was *"difficult to reconcile"* with Article 10.[213] This arguably marks the clear problem with the existing legislation. One cannot promote the freedom of expression in relation to journalists if this freedom is not reserved within the existing legislation.

One cannot also ignore the defences introduced with the update to the 1952 Act contained with section 1 of the Defamation Act 1996, particularly as regards reducing liability for defamation where an individual could show that (a) they were not the author, editor, (b) tool reasonable care and (c) did not know that what he caused contributed to the publication of the defamatory statement. However still the legislation does not deal with the particular idiosyncrasies faced by journalists.

---

[204] 28 DR 77,

[205] 8 EHRR 407

[206] 18 EHRR 276

[207] 19 EHRR 1

[208] 19 EHRR 34

[209] 21 EHRR

[210] 22 EHRR 123

[211] Archbold *op cit* pages 1544-1545

[212] [1980] AC 477 HL

[213] Archbold *op cit* page 1545

In concession journalists although not specifically referred have the benefit of absolute privilege if they pursuant to section 14 of the Defamation Act 1996 if they make a fair and accurate report of judicial proceedings. However the fact that their remains the doctrine of *"qualified privilege at common law"*[214] demonstrates that there is a gap in the existing legislation. Even as in ***Reynold v Times Newspapers Lt****d*[215] and I. Loveland in "Reynolds v Times Newspapers in the House of Lords"[216] however the House of Lords was keen to restrict the protection that Times Newspaper sought in limiting the protection in relation to political speech as not unqualified, but restricted to only certain publications to the world at large. Although arguably the ratio was useful in clarifying the law somewhat, the lack of specific legislation on the point means that in future cases there will be a level of inconsistency over the potential findings, such as occurred *in **Al-Fagih v HH Saudi Research and Marketing (UK) Ltd**.*[217]

In conclusion the law of defamation should be repealed so as to be reconstituted to include the provision that journalists should be given free rein to publish their material without fear of a potential action in defamation. The inconsistencies in the common law justify this course of action and there is space for a Defamation (Journalist exceptions) Act 2010.

---

[214] J, Steele op cit page 783,
[215] [2001] 2 AC 127 I
[216] [2000] PL 351
[217] [2001] EWCA Civ 1634

Chapter 15 - Trespass to a Person

Question

In response to an advertisement in a magazine, Heidi and Rebecca booked, paid for and went to a Murder Mystery weekend. The event was held at the Forest Lodge Hotel in Littlestow. They arrived on Friday evening and met 2 gentlemen for dinner who introduced themselves as Rupert Green and Stephen Sarler. They were also taking part in the Murder Mystery Weekend. After dinner, all the guests who were taking part in the Murder Mystery Weekend's activities gathered in the residents' lounge for a briefing about the event. Rupert and Stephen bought Heidi and Rebecca a drink and they all had a pleasant chat before Rupert and Stephen announced they were going for a walk before going to bed.

Heidi and Rebecca decided to have one final drink before going to bed and had nearly finished when suddenly the lights went out. It was not part of the planned activities as they were not due to start until the next day. Heidi saw a dark figure enter the room and heard a shot fired. Rebecca fainted and collapsed on to the floor. Heidi thought Rebecca had been shot by the intruder. Heidi then saw the dark figure coming towards her and was terrified that she too was about to be shot.

Suddenly the lights went on and Stephen was standing by the door. The intruder turned out to be Rupert who had fired the gun which in fact was a toy gun that could make a loud noise imitating the sound of gunshots. Rupert had decided to play a practical joke in the hope that Heidi and Rebecca would believe the Murder Mystery Weekend had started early.

Whilst Heidi and Rebecca lay on the settee to recover from their ordeal, Jeeves, the night porter, put his hand round the doorway to switch off the lights and to lock the door which he did every night at midnight. He did not see Heidi or Rebecca as they were lying down and he could not see past the back of the settee from his position standing by the door. Heidi and

Rebecca were forced to sleep on the settee all night and were released from the lounge at 7.00am the next morning when Jeeves opened the door.

Advise Heidi and Rebecca on their rights, if any, in the law of tort.

Answer

Introduction

This essay advises Heidi and Rebecca on their rights, if any, in the law of tort. It will discuss the tort of assult on both girls through the practicle joke. It will examine any possible defences that can be raised. It will then discuss the operation of the rule in **Wilkinson v Downton** [1897] 2 QB 57. Lastly, this paper will discuss a possible claim for false imprisonment.

Trespass to the person is an element of tort law which covers wrongs done to an individual. Both Heidi and Rebecca will have a cause of action against Rupert for the tort of assault, because Rupert had decided to play a practical joke in the hope that Heidi and Rebecca would believe the Murder Mystery Weekend had started early. In the law of tort, an assault occurs when a person apprehends immediate and unlawful physical contact. In other words, fearing that you are about to be physically attacked makes you the victim of an assault. It is also necessary that an attack can actually take place. If an attack is impossible, then despite a person's apprehension of physical contact, there can be no assault. Thus if the apprehension of an immediate battery is not possible this will bar an action as in **Thomas v National Union of Mineworkers,** where the picketing miners held back by police and posed no threat of physical contact. This is similar to brandishing an unloaded pistol. This would not be assault, because the Defendant could not have intended battery "There must be the means of carrying the threat into effect" this was highlighted by Tindal CJ in **Stephens v**

Myers (1830) C & P 349. But later in the criminal case of **R v St George** (1840) 9 C&P 483 it was stated that this is an assault. Thus the gist of the tort is to cause a reasonable person to apprehend battery (reasonable person would not know that the gun is unloaded) on an objective test. It can be argued that the girls did not know this was a joke and for them it was very real. Rebecca fainted and collapsed on to the floor. Heidi thought Rebecca had been shot and was terrified that she was also about to be shot. Thus the tort of assult should be actionable.

Moreover, the rule in **Wilkinson v Downton** [1897] 2 QB 57 states where an intentional act (intended to cause distress) causes unintentional consequences, liability may be found (Townshend-Smith: 299). This was approved in **Janvier v Sweeny** [*1919*] 2 KB 316 where the Defendant pretended to be the military authorities with intention of fright; the Claimant suffered severe shock and lost her job. Rupert had decided to play a practical joke in the hope that Heidi and Rebecca would believe the Murder Mystery Weekend had started early. Therefore they could be able to recover compensatory damages as a result of the loss they have sustained.

False imprisonment is the unlawful restraint of a person, which restricts that person's freedom of movement. In order to bring an action under this tort, the victim needs not to be physically restrained from moving. It is sufficient that they are prevented from choosing to go where they please, even if only for a short time (Glasbeek: 77). This includes being forced to stay somewhere, such as in Heidi and Rebecca's situation. A person can also be restrained, even if they have means of escape but it is unreasonable for them to take it, for example, if they have no clothes or they are in a first floor room with only a window as a way out. False imprisonment can also be committed if the victim is unaware that they are being restrained, but it must be a fact that they are being restrained. The ingredients for false imprisonment are complete restraint e.g. it will not be complete if the claimant can leave or is able to escape as in **Wright v Wilson** [1699] 1 Ld Raym 73. The restrain must be intentional, but malice is not necessary as in **R v Governor of Brockhill Prison (No 2)** [2001] 2 AC 19. It is not necessary that the Claimants are imprisoned. Confinement of some type will suffice. **Burton v Davies** considered the issue of assault and false imprisonment and whether or not a woman was assaulted and falsely imprisoned, when the Defendant drove at high speed which prevented her from exiting the vehicle. By using this case, we can advise that the girls were forced to sleep in the bar area, with no exit, which will meet the criteria required. Actual knowledge by the Claimant of detention is not necessary. Only proof of total restraint is required as per **Murray v Ministry of Defence** [1988] 2 All ER 521. Both girls seem to have an action for faulse imprisonment. Jeeves, the night porter, locked the door. Heidi and Rebecca were forced to sleep on the settee all night and and were released from the lounge at 7. 00 am the next morning when Jeeves opened the door. The legnth of time of their restraint will not matter, it will be actionable "for however short a time" as said in **Bird v Jonesn** (1845) 115 ER 668.

Chapter 16 - Remedies

Problem Question

Precision Implants Plc ["Precision"] is a UK manufacturer of medical implants, including hip joint replacements that incorporate tantalum, a rare mineral. Tantalum increases the non-corrosive properties of metal alloys to which it is added. Precision's main supplier of tantalum is Ngualla Minerals Ltd [Ngualla], a company based in Tanzania which extracts and processes tantalum and ships it globally.

In 2012 Abasi joined Precision's procurement department, based at its factory near Slough, England, after working for Ngualla in Dares Salaam, Tanzania. At Ngualla, Abasi worked closely with Bado, an ambitious manager, who was at that time head of quality control at Ngualla.

Abasi's position at Precision gives Abasi access to all arrangements for supply and delivery of substances that go into the manufacturing process for all of Precision's medical implant products.

Precision's hip joint implants had been considered market leading on quality because they incorporate 99% pure tantalum powder. However, beginning in 2013, failure reports and other complaints from Precision's health service clients about hip joint implants began to rise.

Last week, Sumiko, who is a Director at Precision, was assigned to investigate the problem. In the factory storeroom she discovered that two cases marked "99% pure tantalum powder", in fact, contained a mixture of tantalum and another unidentified mineral and were labelled for shipment to a warehouse in west London.

Sumiko tried to contact Bado to question him about any quality tests on tantalum powder recently shipped from Ngualla to Precision, but learned that Bado was summarily dismissed 3 months ago and is believed to be working in Bejing as a consultant for a Chinese state owned mineral trading company.

Sumiko drove to the warehouse near to the location of which she noticed a new Mercedes car similar to one she recently saw Abasi driving into Precision's factory car park. She also noticed a van nearby from Top Tech Ltd. Sumiko recognised Top Tech Ltd as a firm supplying technical support for 3D printers used to manufacture some medical implants.

Sumiko then discovered that Abasi had applied for holiday leave and booked two one-way airline tickets to Bejing, leaving the day after tomorrow. On the same day, a laptop computer owned by Precision was signed out by Zuri, an administrator in Precision's product design department. The laptop has not been returned and Zuri went on sick leave the day she signed out the computer. The laptop may have contained confidential documents, including detailed patented designs for hip joint implants and other products and Precision customer details. Sumiko has heard office gossip that Zuri recently left her husband and moved into a flat in Chelsea in London purchased by Abasi, but that the flat had recently been put on the market and a sale had already been agreed.

Sumiko knows Abasi's salary, which is paid into an account at a branch of Big Bank in Chelsea, and is doubtful that he could easily afford to purchase either the car or the flat.

Sumiko suspects Abasi, Zuri and possibly Bado, of conspiring to manufacture and sell inferior versions of Precision hip joint implants using diluted tantalum stolen from Precision, passing off the fake implants as Precision's products. She thinks that they may be moving the operation and their profits out of the UK imminently.

Assume that Precision have a potential cause of action against Abasi, Zuri and possibly Bado. Do not discuss the merits of the cause of action.

Advise Precision as to whether there are any available equitable remedies that may assist them in determining quickly whether Sumiko's theory is correct, in recovering or securing their property and in making sure that they can recover damages against Abasi if their claim is ultimately successful.

Answer

Introduction

This is an advice for Precision as to whether any equitable remedies can be used to assist them in recovering or securing their property. First, this advice will discuss how to prevent them from selling inferior parts. Second, how to recover damages through the remedy of account. Third, it will look at search and freezing orders to located money and stop it from being dissipated.

Equitable remedies

Sumiko suspects that Abasi, Zuri and possibly Bado, are conspiring to manufacture and sell inferior versions of Precision hip joint implants, passing off the fake implants and moving the operation and their profits out of the UK imminently. Assuming that Precision have a potential cause of action there are two things that can be done. First, they can apply to the courts for an interim injunction from stopping them from passing off and using information relation to Precision and second they can ask Abasi, Zuri and possibly Bado, to account for profits.

Interim Injunction

The general principle is that an injunction can be sought. This Order of the court prohibits and prevents a person to perform a particular act i.e. of passing off and using trade secrets. The injunction is a remedy *in personam*. This means it is a personal remedy and not a propriety one. Precision can apply to the High Court under Section 37(1) of the Supreme Court Act 1981. The guidelines used by the courts for the granting of interim injunctions are couched in the case of **American Cyanamid Co v Ethicon Ltd.**[218] Injunctions are discretionary because they are equitable and the courts will consider the **American Cyanamid** in deciding whether to grant an injunction and exercise its equitable discretion. Firstly, the court must satisfy itself that Precision's case is not "frivolous or vexatious". This means that there is "a serious question to be tried".[219] We are told to assume that Precision have a potential cause of action for the information being used to pass off the fake implants as Precision's products. This is a real issue between the parties to be settled at trial and Precision have *some* prospect of success.[220]

Second, if the court deems that there is a serious issue to be tired, they then go on to consider "whether the balance of convenience lies in favour of granting or refusing" the interim injunction.[221] This entails the court engaging in a balancing exercise to assess the minimisation of risk of doing injustice. The leaking of the information is leaking of trade secrets and passing off can be quite damaging to Precision.

Third, the court will go on to consider if either party could be adequately compensated by an award of damages instead. This means the court will consider if they refuse an injunction and the Precision wins at trial, whether Abasi, Zuri Bado can adequately compensated them through damages for any loss caused by their actions before the trial. If so, and Abasi, Zuri and possibly Bado would be in a position to pay, then the interim injunction will be refused by the court. Alternatively the court will consider if the injunction sought is granted and if Precision loses at trial, then can Abasi, Zuri and possibly

---

[218] [1975] AC 396

[219] Gray, Christine. "Interlocutory Injunctions since Cyanamid." The Cambridge Law Journal 40.02 (1981): 307-339.

[220] **Mothercare v Robson Books** [1975] FSR 466

[221] Martin, Jill. "Interlocutory Injunctions: American Cyanamid comes of Age." KCLJ 4 (1993): 52.

Bado be adequately compensated by the Precision's undertaking to pay damages for the granting interim injunction.

Other relevant matters affecting the granting of the injunction is the balance of convenience. Lord Diplock stated that "it would be unwise to attempt even to list all the various matters which may be taken into consideration"[222] but things the court have considered important which are relevant to Precision include damage to the goodwill of a business[223] the closing down of a business;[224] and preserving a substantial investment.[225] This factor will be relevant in granting the injunction, because the passing off is causing damage to their business. In 2013, failure reports and other complaints from Precision's health service clients about hip joint implants began to rise.

Moreover, the court may consider special factors in the balance of convenience test, if particular circumstances exist. Where the balance of convenience test is not conclusive and does not favour one party over the other, the factor which decides if an injunction will be granted is "the preservation of the status quo". Moreover, as a test of last resort the court can examine the merits of the case. However, the court will not be inclined to consider the merits of the case unless the balance of convenience is not conclusive.

Accounting

Secondly, Abasi, Zuri and possibly Bado have all played a part and could be working together to make a profit. They can all be seen as fiduciaries (individuals that have a duty of trusts and loyalty) that can be made to account to Precision for any incidental profit they have made outside of their employment

---

[222] [1975] AC 396 at p408

[223] **Associated Newspapers plc v Insert Media Ltd** [1991] 1 WLR 571

[224] **Potters-Ballotini Ltd v Weston-Baker** [1977] RPC 202

[225] **Catnic Components Ltd v Stressline Ltd** [1976] FSR 157

in breach of their fiduciary duties.[226] Moreover, they could all be made to account as agents or fiduciaries to account for any bribes or secret profit[227] that they have made in Beijing. Additionally Abasi, Zuri and possibly Bado could be made to account as a person to account for profits for the unauthorised use of information in breach of confidence.[228] In these authorities cited account seems to be used as a substantive remedy. One problem will be locating the money which may be outside of the jurisdiction. One solution might be a search order to determine where the monies are being kept.[229]

Search Order

This is a mandatory injunction which will allow Precision to enter Abasi, Zuri and possibly Bado's premises (business or residential) to search for and inspect photographs, statements, documents, or records and allow Precision to remove such evidence for trial.[230] Any failure to comply with the order will be seen as a contempt of court (this could lead to imprisonment of Abasi, Zuri and possibly Bado) and likely to lead to adverse inferences being drawn at the trial as in **Anton Piller KG v Manufacturing Processes Ltd**[231]. This can be used to stop Zuri from leaking information on the laptop. Moreover, such an order may shed some light on where the money is being kept and after its whereabouts has been located a freezing injection can be sought.

---

[226] **Williams v Barton** [1927] 2 Ch 9, **Boardman v Phipps** [1967] 2 AC 46
[227] **A-G for Hong Kong v Reid** [1994] 1 All ER 1
[228] **Her Majesty's Attorney-General v Guardian Newspapers Ltd (No 2)** [1988] 3 All ER 545 (the Spycatcher case); **Her Majesty's Attorney-General v Blake** [2000] 4 All ER 385
[229] Eichengrun, Joel. "Remedying the Remedy of Accounting" Ind. LJ 60 (1984): 463.
[230] Staines, Anne. "Protection of Intellectual Property Rights: Anton Piller Orders." The Modern Law Review 46.3 (1983): 274-288.
[231] [1976] Ch 55

Freezing injunction

Sumiko knows Abasi's salary, which is paid into an account at a branch of Big Bank in Chelsea, and is doubtful that he could easily afford to purchase either the car or the flat. As precision know the details of his bank account, this can be used to locate money for the remedy of account. This is a prohibitory injunction which will order Abasi, Zuri and possibly Bado not to dispose of or remove their assets from the jurisdiction before trial and prevent them from defeating the effectiveness of any judgment in the Precision's favour.[232] The freezing order is an equitable remedy which also acts *in personam*. A freezing injunction will not have any effect on the assest itself just its use and transference. Abasi, Zuri and Bado could still *physically* deal with their assets under a freezing injunction, but this would put them in contempt of the court Order. In the case of **Nippon Yusen Kaisha v Karageorgisi**,[233] which was followed in **Mareva Compagnia Naviera SA v International Bulkcarriers SA**[234], the Court of Appeal led by Lord Denning, M.R., coined the **Mareva** injunction as, "the greatest piece of judicial law reform in my time."[235] The Jurisdiction is now governed by Section 37 of the Supreme Court Act 1981 and such relief may be granted where, "it appears to the court to be just and convenient to do so". However, the requirements of a freezing Order are stricter than for other interim injunctions. Precision must, show according, to **Derby & Co Ltd v Weldon**,[236] that first there is a case with merit. Second, Abasi, Zuri and Bado have assets within the jurisdiction (an extra-territorial order can be sought); and third, a real risk that they will be removed or dissipated exists. Moreover, an ancillary to the Order, the court may grant an order requiring disclosure of the Abasi, Zuri and Bado assets and their whereabouts.

---

[232] Rein, Eric S. "International Fraud: Freeze, Seize, and Retrieve." Banking LJ 116 (1999): 144.
[233] [1975] 3 All ER 282
[234] [1975], 2 Lloyd's Rep. 509
[235] Denning, 'The Due Process of Law' (1980, Butterworths)
[236] [1990] Ch 48